Globalization and the Poor

This book attempts to save globalization from both its critics and its advocates. The argument the author presents is that globalization is associated with the economic growth necessary to alleviate poverty. Globalization therefore should be encouraged. At the same time, however, governments must adopt policies that address the needs of those who are victimized by the dislocations caused by the process. The book thus responds to the opponents by emphasizing globalization's potential to alleviate poverty but is at the same time critical of those who defend globalization without acknowledging the costs it imposes on innocent victims. In addressing the activist opponents of the process, the author maintains that they should not reject the global integration of world markets out of a concern for justice. Instead of either turning against globalization or advocating United States unilateralism in shaping the global economy, activists can advance the interests of the world's poor by mounting political movements to promote international agreements to stabilize the world economy and ensure labor rights.

Jay R. Mandle has been W. Bradford Wiley Professor of Economics at Colgate University since 1990. Before that he taught at Temple University, as well as at universities in China, Trinidad and Tobago, Guyana, and Barbados. He has received two Fulbright Scholar awards and written numerous books and articles on Caribbean economic development, African-American economic history, and economic growth.

Globalization and the Poor

JAY R. MANDLE
Colgate University

CAMBRIDGE
UNIVERSITY PRESS

PUBLISHED BY THE PRESS SYNDICATE OF THE UNIVERSITY OF CAMBRIDGE
The Pitt Building, Trumpington Street, Cambridge, United Kingdom

CAMBRIDGE UNIVERSITY PRESS
The Edinburgh Building, Cambridge CB2 2RU, UK
40 West 20th Street, New York, NY 10011-4211, USA
477 Williamstown Road, Port Melbourne, VIC 3207, Australia
Ruiz de Alarcón 13, 28014 Madrid, Spain
Dock House, The Waterfront, Cape Town 8001, South Africa

http://www.cambridge.org

© Jay R. Mandle 2003

First published 2003

Printed in the United States of America

Typeface Sabon 10.5/15 pt.   *System* QuarkXPress [BTS]

A catalog record for this book is available from the British Library.

Library of Congress Cataloging in Publication Data
Mandle, Jay R.
Globalization and the poor / Jay R. Mandle.
p.   cm.
Includes bibliographical references and index.
ISBN 0-521-81504-5 (hardback) – ISBN 0-521-89352-6 (pbk.)
1. International economic relations.   2. Globalization – Economic aspects.
3. Poverty – Government policy.   I. Title.
HF 1359 .M356 2002
337 – dc21   2002020165

ISBN   0 521 81504 5   hardback
ISBN   0 521 89352 6   paperback

To Anna,
in the hope that she
will join the struggle for
a more just world.

Contents

vii

Preface

I would prefer to allow the argument of this book to stand on its own, without reference to my personal experiences. Yet I would be remiss if I failed to explain to readers that though I am very much an American, I have spent much of my professional life living in and studying countries where the standard of living is much lower than that of the United States. It is for this reason that I, perhaps more than most, appreciate and prize the accomplishment that economic development represents.

Economic development creates better lives for the people who experience it. Because that is so, the premise of this book is that modern economic growth (to use the phrase of the late Nobel laureate Simon Kuznets) is desirable, and that policies and institutions impeding that process should be opposed. My sense is that what separates me from many fellow activists is the priority that I place on the urgency of achieving economic modernization.

To be sure, there is much to be alarmed at in the way the United States uses its wealth, and certainly by advocating economic modernization I am not endorsing a universal replication of this country. Nevertheless, I believe that the application of modern science and technology to production is necessary if the lives of poor people are to be improved. Because I think that, economic development, for me, assumes the status of a moral imperative. I further believe that democracy itself requires development. Impoverished people, by definition, do not possess the resources necessary to be effective participants in a deliberative democracy.

Over the years, both family and friends have been subjected to my frequent discourses on this subject. This circle has grown through marriage, birth, and "adoption," and with that growth I too have been stretched. Joan Mandle, Jon Mandle, Karen Schupack, and Adonal Foyle have all helped me by listening to my ideas and challenging me in response. Anna Schupack has not yet offered a political retort to my presentations, though even at her tender age she is a source of renewed inspiration. Lou Ferleger, Paul Lyons, Pat Burke, Mike Burke, and Iz Reivich are my most long-standing discussion partners – a group that in recent years has been joined by Adam Weinberg and Anne Weinberg. And, of course, I am constantly stimulated and provoked by students in my economic development classes, particularly those in the seminar on the subject that I teach at Colgate University.

Lew Bateman at Cambridge University Press was supportive of this project from beginning to end. The fact that this book falls between disciplinary boundaries was never a problem for him, and his tolerance of its resulting idiosyncrasies allowed me to develop my argument without worrying that what I had to say was not pure economics, or sociology, or political science. At the Press I have been served well by two anonymous referees who offered valuable substantive suggestions, as well as by production editor Russell Hahn, production controller Susanna Fry, and editorial assistant Lauren Levin. Susan Greenberg unraveled my prose in her role as copyeditor, and Glorieux Dougherty delved deeply into the meaning of the text in developing the index for this volume.

ONE

Introduction

The benefits of globalization, write Albert Fishlow and Karen Parker, are many:

> [T]elevision sets, microwaves, automobiles, and computers have become less expensive and more reliable. Were it not for job creation in the high-wage export and technology sectors, the slowdown in U.S. productivity and earnings would likely have been greater. The evidence suggests that foreign direct investment has contributed to the growth of U.S. exports, which are produced with more advanced technologies by higher-skill, better-paid workers. To the extent that trade augments competition and expands potential markets, productivity is enhanced, although economists debate the degree of change. (Fishlow and Parker 1999, 9)

Their position represents the consensus among economists concerning globalization. Taken as a whole, global market integration is seen as a desirable process, one that helps to advance worldwide living standards.

However, an important anti-globalization movement in the United States rejects this view. Instead, it sees in globalization a process that should be abandoned or radically altered. These activists think of globalization as possessing overwhelmingly negative social consequences. They believe that its impetus derives from the greed of multinational corporations and that its benefits accrue almost exclusively to the already rich. Barbara Ehrenreich captures the voice of this opposition when she writes that "wherever globalization impinges, inequality deepens. From Mexico to Japan, the rich are getting richer while the poor are becoming more desperate and numerous" (Ehrenreich 2000, x).

In the past, at least a segment of the opposition to capitalist globalization would have responded by advocating an internationalist socialism. For these critics, the global economy, excluding the communist bloc, would have been understood as an economic system in which private decision makers – in this instance multinational corporations – enrich themselves while inflicting deprivation on most of the rest of the population. These opponents of globalization would have found nothing wrong with a technology that permitted the worldwide integration of economic activity. Rather, they would have argued that such a technology could be beneficial, but only if it were deployed in a socialist setting, introduced to advance public welfare rather than private wealth accumulation.

An appeal to socialism, however, is no longer politically tenable. One reason for this is that socialism has been tarred by the oppression and tyranny practiced in its name in the former Soviet Union and its allies. But in addition, the socialism of the communist countries proved to be ineffective in employing modern technologies. In particular, advanced methods of processing information, communicating, and accessing knowledge never took root, even during the years of Soviet ascendancy. Because of this failure, the positing of socialism as an economic system in which globalization – a process that is nothing if not technologically driven – could flourish is not credible. Anti-globalization activists of the left therefore cannot advance the same vision that animated radicals in the past: an international commonwealth of cooperating economies in which decisions are motivated not by private interests but by the goal of advancing the public's well-being. Of great importance in this regard is that efforts by left intellectuals to define a "feasible socialism" in which markets and private firms play an important role, such as in Alec Nove's discussion of the subject, have not achieved political resonance (Nove 1983).

Nevertheless, an important activist opposition to globalization has emerged. In the absence of socialism as a unifying objective, it is not really surprising that this opposition has failed to come to a consensus on what should be proposed as an alternative to globalization. According to Jeff Faux, himself a critic of the process, "As with most parties in opposition, the coalition partners most agree on what they don't want" (Faux 1999, 5, 6).

Despite this lack of consensus, it is possible to identify three principal viewpoints within the activist opposition to globalization. The advocacy of United States unilateralism is one such position, and the call for the economics of localism is another. The third position, that of the student anti-sweatshop movement, shares the anti-global sensibility of the other two but does so without fitting easily in either camp.

The advocates of United States unilateralism believe that before allowing poor countries to trade with it, the United States should insist that they agree to labor, environmental, and human rights standards. The intention is to use American power to accomplish such desirable goals as raising wages, encouraging unions, and advancing human rights. The advocates of localism take a different tack, rejecting the concept of a global economy altogether. In this, they take their lead from Wolfgang Sachs, who believes that "development was a misconceived enterprise from the beginning" and that "the time is ripe to write its obituary" (Sachs 1996, 3, 1). Viewing globalization as the logical extension of development, these critics call for a reversal of the process and a movement to greater local self-sufficiency. Finally, the anti-sweatshop movement, in contrast to both of these efforts, has a more limited objective. It seeks to improve the wages and working conditions present in the third world's apparel industry. To do so it seeks to mobilize support both in the United States and abroad in order to pressure producers to pay higher wages and eliminate unsafe work environments.

Neither the unilateralists nor the localists offer an attractive alternative, particularly if the objective is to alleviate human deprivation. In contrast, while its objectives are desirable, the student movement almost certainly lacks the resources to accomplish them.

Because it would be fiercely opposed by other countries, United States unilateralism would more likely hamstring than advance international trade in particular and globalization in general. The problem is that if agreement on standards could not be reached and trade with third world nations really were curtailed, the people most harmed would be the working class and the poor in those nations, especially those people displaced from employment in export industries. The advocates of localism appear to be similarly indifferent to the costs their strategy would impose on the hopes of the world's poor to achieve rising living standards. They simply leave unanswered how income levels might rise in a world in which economic development is rejected and flows of capital, resources, and knowledge are impeded.

Of course, not all progressives subscribe to these positions. Robert Reich, the former United States secretary of labor, believes that "free trade and global capital are essentially good things if managed correctly" (Reich 1999, 17). Even Ehrenreich would not turn her back entirely on globalization. She remarks that "potentially globalization could lead to a safer, more peaceful and – who knows? – more interesting world," and as a result she warns that "the solution does not lie in a retreat to nationalism and rigid protectionism or hermetically sealed economies like that of North Korea" (Ehrenreich 2000, x).

Nevertheless, many liberals and radicals either are skeptical about globalization or actually oppose the process. I accept neither stance despite my sharing their concerns about justice and equality; with regard to those goals, I too am an activist. I, however, believe that in failing to affirm the desirability of globalization the critics have placed themselves in an untenable opposition to a process of immense potential benefit to the world's poor. Advancing the interests of disadvantaged populations does not require that globalization be abandoned or that the process be shaped unilaterally by the United States. Accomplishing that goal requires, instead, interventionist policies implemented at the national level to ensure that the benefits associated with globalization are shared equitably. Needed are policies to maintain worker income and benefits when globalization results in job losses, to educate and retrain people for the new opportunities created by globalization, and to assist retrained workers seeking new employment. In short, globalization should be reformed, not rejected or frustrated by a certain-to-be-resented exercise of unilateral power by the United States.

What I will argue for – and what differentiates my argument from those who follow anti-globalists like Ralph Nader, Lori Wallach, and others – is my belief that within globalization there remains ample room for ameliorative policies. Furthermore, where global agreements are required, nothing like the American impositions that United States liberals call for are needed. Those who seek social justice have much work to do in shaping globalization. But this goal is not achieved by maintaining either that the potential latent in modern technology is undesirable or that the United States has a unique ability or interest in governing globalization in the name of fairness.

My argument is presented in the next seven chapters. In Chapter 2 I take up the relationship between globalization and the

reduction of poverty in third world countries, arguing that globalization is an important means by which to achieve that goal. I
then discuss in Chapter 3 the sources of the opposition to globalization. In doing so, I take to task the advocates of trade openness. Those who have promoted increased trade have generally
failed to pay sufficient attention to the negative dislocations associated with the process. They therefore have also failed to emphasize the need for policies to reduce the burdens that accompany
the economic restructuring that globalization induces. In responding to this failing, the activist community has drawn the wrong
lesson, namely, that to overlook the problems caused by its spread
is inherent in globalization and therefore is inevitable. But as I
argue, globalization does not require laissez-faire policies, and
social neglect is not invariably embedded in the process. The third
and fourth chapters subject both unilateralism and localization to
criticism. In the fifth chapter I examine the now-abandoned project
to negotiate a multilateral agreement on investment (MAI). I
discuss my objections to the MAI as well as the failed effort to
come to an agreement. I also examine criticisms raised by the
project's opponents. I maintain that while the "deep integration"
of the MAI was almost certainly beyond reach, a "bottom-up
approach," though much less ambitious, might have played a
useful role in rationalizing flows of foreign direct investment (FDI).
In Chapter 6 I discuss the financial volatility present in contemporary globalization and the problems caused in particular by "hot
money." I contend that a global agreement to constrain "hot
money" is both needed and feasible. In Chapter 7 the issue of labor
in the global economy is addressed with an analysis of the student
anti-sweatshop movement. My view is that instead of confining
themselves to collaborating with non-governmental organizations
(NGOs) in poor countries, students would be better advised to
mount a political movement to strengthen the International Labor
Organization (ILO) and in that way increase the likelihood that

6

workers in poor countries will be able to defend their own interests without external patronage. A final chapter reviews policies that could be adopted to make globalization both more efficient and more equitable.

TWO

Economic Globalization and the Development of Poor Nations

The era of globalization is set off from the past by the distinctiveness of its technologies. As Thomas L. Friedman puts it, globalization is driven by "computerization, miniaturization, digitization, satellite communications, fiber optics and the Internet" (Friedman 1999, 8). Because they "permit instantaneous communication among the far-flung operations of global enterprises," these technologies, in conjunction with the development of new materials and production processes and improvements in sea and air transportation, have "created and mandated greater interdependence among firms and nations" (Stever and Muroyama 1988, 1). With these innovations, the potential for global economic integration is greater than it has ever been before.

But the spread of globalization is not, as Friedman believes, as inevitable as the fact that "the sun comes up every morning" (Friedman 1999, xviii). Rather, the global spread of production requires that beyond the availability of the new technology two additional conditions be satisfied. A liberal international trading system is needed, as is a relatively well-educated labor force. When those are in place, the new systems of communication, information processing, and control allow profitable production to be carried out virtually anywhere: no country is so remote that investors will be dissuaded by location alone. Because that is so, modern production methods can be introduced into countries that previously were by-passed by economic development.

By conceptualizing globalization in this way I am differentiating my usage from that of Kevin O'Rourke and Jeffrey Williamson. They are right to remind us that international economic integration is not unique to the late twentieth century. From the middle of the nineteenth century to the beginning of World War I, the ties between economies on both sides of the Atlantic had become closer as international trade and foreign investment grew to historically high levels (O'Rourke and Williamson 1999, 2).

But while it is useful to point to the historical antecedents of contemporary globalization, the similarities between the phenomenon in the nineteenth century and the process underway at present can be overdrawn. In particular, the geographic scope of what occurred in the first period was significantly narrower than it is at present. In the nineteenth century, participation in the international economy was confined largely to Europe and to regions of settlement by Europeans such as North America. Because globalization was delimited in this way, its positive impact was also confined. Today, in contrast, the extent of geographic inclusion in the international economy is much wider, involving parts of Latin America, Asia, and Africa that formerly had been either omitted altogether or, as occurred with formal colonialism, only partially integrated.

Because globalization represents something that is historically unique, it is misleading to maintain, as Louis Uchitelle quips in the *New York Times*, that "when it comes to globalization, the 20th century is ending on a note of deja vu: the world's economies are roughly as intertwined today as they were in 1913" (Uchitelle 1998, 1). What is going on today is something that is inadequately captured by the measures of globalization Uchitelle employs: the growth rate of trade and foreign direct investment as a percentage of world output. His formulation misses what is distinctive in today's experience. Only in recent decades, as Robert Pollin has remarked, are "we . . . moving in the direction of every country being able to produce everything" (quoted in Uchitelle 1998, 1).

TRADE LIBERALIZATION

Since World War II, substantial advances have been achieved in trade liberalization. According to Anne O. Krueger, gains during these years "far exceeded what any of those planning the system could have reasonably hoped for" (Krueger 1998, 4). Between the immediate postwar years and the mid-1990s, global tariff levels fell from about 20 percent of the value of imports to about 5 percent. Important exceptions to this pattern remained; nonetheless, as Bordo, Eichengreen, and Irwin write, "broadly speaking, trade barriers have fallen substantially in the postwar period and today are quite likely lower than they were a century ago" (Bordo, Eichengreen, and Irwin 1999, 17).

Krueger points however to the irony that, until the establishment of the World Trade Organization (WTO) in 1995, this liberalization occurred "even though the nations participating in deliberations over the postwar international economic system were unable to produce a charter for an international trade organization that was acceptable to key governments" (Krueger 1998, 2–3). In the years immediately after World War II, the proposed International Trade Organization (ITO) had been thought of as such an organization. But formation of the ITO was opposed by business groups in the United States. According to Eckes, these groups worried that the new organization "would prove too bureaucratic, too tolerant of exchange and trade restrictions and too much a forum for developing and debtor countries." At the time, the National Association of Manufacturers objected to the charter of the ITO because it would make the world "safe for socialistic plan-ning" and thus a "very precarious place" for private enterprise (Eckes 1999, 74).

Because the ITO never came to fruition, post–World War II trade negotiations were carried on without a formal sponsoring organization. Instead, the process of reducing tariffs was initiated in 1947 when the United States invited nineteen countries to negotiate bilateral trade agreements on a product-by-product basis. These agreements became the multilateral General Agree-ment on Tariffs and Trade (GATT), which became operative on January 1, 1948.

Under the GATT umbrella, eight rounds of trade negotiations were held between 1947 and 1994. In the early rounds (1949, 1950–51, 1956, and 1960–62), negotiations were conducted on the original bilateral product-by-product basis. However, starting with the Kennedy Round (1962–67) multilateral negotiations were initiated, and additional countries were admitted into the nego-tiating process. By early 1995, when GATT finally came to an end, the original 19 participating nations had become 128, which included nearly the entire world of sovereign nations.

The GATT did not establish truly free trade. Signatories to the GATT were not compelled to reduce their tariffs to zero. Instead, in the GATT process, nations were called upon to negotiate mutual tariff reductions with their chief trading partners. Once these downward adjustments had been made, the terms of the GATT agreement stipulated that participating countries extend those same – reduced – tariffs to all other participants. This was described as the extension of most favored nation privileges. Not only were the new tariff levels made available to all signatories in this way, but the nations involved also agreed to hold the tariffs at the new lower level – referred to as "binding" the tariffs. Numerous exceptions and exemptions to these principles were per-mitted under the terms of the GATT. Nevertheless, trade became

increasingly liberalized, permitting it to expand rapidly throughout the period. Krueger explains that "the key principle to which
the GATT contracting parties subscribed was an open and nondis-
criminatory trade, thus giving rise to the term 'open multilateral
system'" (Krueger 1998, 4).

POOR COUNTRIES AND TRADE LIBERALIZATION

Through the 1970s many of the leaders of the third world believed
that their nations could achieve development only by disengaging
from, not integrating into, the global economy. Skeptical of international trade as a source of development, numerous poor countries adopted policies of import substitution industrialization (ISI).
They sought to industrialize by replacing imports with domestically produced manufactured goods. Little emphasis was placed
on exports. Only after the Asian Tigers of Singapore, Hong Kong,
South Korea, and Taiwan achieved phenomenally high growth
rates by emphasizing exports during the 1970s, was a movement
away from the ISI consensus initiated. Increasingly, the nations of
the developing world, in pursuit of accelerated growth rates,
adopted policies to increase their participation in global markets
(Coclanis and Doshi 2000, 57).

Most of the third world remained aloof from the negotiations
organized by the GATT. To the extent that they did engage in international trade diplomacy, most poor countries directed their efforts
to obtaining preferential access to the markets of the developed
world on a unilateral, non-reciprocal basis. Diplomatic successes
in this regard included the Generalized System of Preferences (GSP)
and the series of Lomé Agreements reached between the seventy
countries of the African, Caribbean, and Pacific grouping of countries (ACP) and the European Community. But the payoff for
these efforts in terms of expanding trade was limited. According
to Kreuger, "most analysts believe that, although GSP had some

value to developing countries, it was limited to a few countries and a few commodities [and that] it may not have been worth even the diplomatic efforts and other costs to developing countries" (Kreuger 1995, 40).

Despite the absence of most of the third world from the GATT trade negotiations, those talks did result in the opening of markets for products made in poor countries. To the extent that the principles of reduced tariffs and non-discrimination were agreed to and were implemented, even countries that had stayed aloof from the GATT talks gained in their access to markets. But there were major exceptions to this liberalizing trend that adversely affected poor nations. The Multifiber Arrangement limited textile imports to the developed countries, as did protectionist policies with regard to agricultural goods. In spite of this GATT produced an increasingly favorable global trade environment. As Jagdish Bhagwati puts it, "the GATT trading system has achieved unprecedented trade expansion and world prosperity" (Bhagwati 1998, 271).

RESTRUCTURING THE GLOBAL ECONOMY

The availability of the new technologies and the more liberal trade environment created by the GATT process were not sufficient by themselves to accelerate development in poor nations or to increase the importance of such nations in the global economy. In addition, those nations needed to achieve advances in the educational attainment of their people. The technologies associated with globalization require workers to have a relatively high level of schooling before they can use the technologies efficiently. This is not primarily a question of the engineers who design the new instruments of communications and control. Rather, it concerns the literacy and numeracy skills that are necessary to work with those new tools. As the World Bank points out, "a growing economy, even a low-income one, needs people with up-to-date technical skills to participate in the global economy" (World Bank 1998–99, 8). For the new technology to be efficiently used, people must be competent.

Though they lag behind developed nations, the poor nations of the world increasingly possess such competence. In its *World Development Report* for 1998–99, the World Bank expresses satisfaction that "in the past 30 years, developing countries have made enormous strides in expanding enrollments at all levels, particularly in primary school" (World Bank 1998–99, 8). Thus, among the thirteen largest underdeveloped countries, the population-weighted school enrollment rate increased between 1980 and 1996 from 37.5 to 57.5 percent, while illiteracy fell from 19.0 to 12.4 percent for men and from 36.4 to 22.0 percent for women (Table 2.1). By no means do these data indicate that the gap in educational attainment between the developed countries and the less developed ones has been closed, nor of course do they suggest that the disadvantage experienced by women compared to men has been eliminated. Nevertheless, it is clear that educational achievement in poor countries has improved, enabling increased numbers of people in those nations to participate more effectively in production processes that employ the new technology.

Poor countries therefore have become increasingly attractive locations for manufacturers to undertake production. Wages are lower than in the developed world, and the bottleneck of a skills shortage is less burdensome. Indeed, dating from the 1980s, the world has seen a dramatic change in the role played in the international economy by underdeveloped nations, particularly the larger ones. Krueger has estimated that 3 percent of total exported manufactured goods originated in developing countries in 1970. Twenty years later, in 1990, that share stood at 18 percent (Krueger 1995, 43). No longer are countries such as Bangladesh, India, or Thailand largely self-contained, limiting their exports to raw materials and agricultural goods. As shown in Table 2.2, which lists

TABLE 2.1. Secondary school enrollment rates and youth illiteracy rates, selected large poor countries (percent)

| | Population (Millions) | Secondary School Enrollment Rate | | Youth Illiteracy Rate | | | |
| | | | | M | | F | |
		1980	1996	1980	1997	1980	1997
Bangladesh	126	18	NA	52	42	74	63
Brazil	166	13	45	15	10	13	7
China	1,239	46	70	4	1	16	4
Egypt	61	51	75	36	25	62	41
Ethiopia	61	9	12	59	47	78	51
India	980	30	49	32	23	61	44
Indonesia	204	29	48	7	2	15	4
Mexico	96	49	61	6	3	9	5
Nigeria	121	18	33	32	13	57	20
Pakistan	132	14	NA	48	31	79	61
Philippines	75	64	77	5	2	5	2
Thailand	61	29	56	3	1	4	2
Turkey	63	35	56	6	2	25	8
POPULATION-WEIGHTED MEAN		37.5	57.5	19.0	12.4	36.4	22.0

Sources: Population: World Bank, *World Development Report 1999/2000* (New York: Oxford University Press 1999), Table 1; Secondary School Enrollment Rate: World Bank, *World Development Indicators, 1999* (Washington, DC: World Bank, 1999), Table 2.10; Youth Illiteracy, Rate: *World Development Indicators 1999*, Table 2.11.

thirteen large underdeveloped countries, in eight of the eleven for which data are available for 1997, manufactures represent at least 50 percent of total exports. In 1980 that had been the case for only two of those countries.

TABLE 2.2. Manufactures as percentage of merchandise
exports, selected large poor countries, 1980, 1997

	1980	1997	Change
Bangladesh	68	87	+19
Brazil	37	54	+17
China	NA	NA	NA
Egypt	11	40	+29
Ethiopia	NA	66	NA
India	59	72	+13
Indonesia	2	42	+40
Mexico	12	81	+69
Nigeria	0	NA	NA
Pakistan	48	86	+38
Philippines	21	45	+24
Thailand	25	71	+46
Turkey	27	75	+48
POPULATION-WEIGHTED MEAN	44	68	+24

Source: World Bank, World Development Indicators 1999, Table 4.5.

The impact of this export breakthrough for the large poor
countries is shown in Table 2.3, which gives the growth rates
of the economies and of exports for the thirteen largest underdeveloped countries for three periods: 1950–73, 1973–92, and
1990–98. What is clear from this table is that exports from these
nations accelerated during the 1973–92 period and that the
upward trend continued during the 1990s. Simultaneously, the
pace of economic growth also picked up. To be sure, this table
does not show causality; even if the growth in exports did contribute to the economic growth of these countries, international
trade was not the only factor involved. Nevertheless, the association between exports and economic growth is unmistakable. We

TABLE 2.3. Population-weighted mean annual rates of growth of exports and gross domestic product (GDP), selected large poor countries, 1950–73, 1973–92, 1990–98

	Exports (Percent)	GDP (Percent)
1950–73	3.4	4.7
1973–92	7.3	5.3
1990–98	12.0	7.3

Sources: Exports: 1950–73 and 1973–92, Maddison, Tables 3–10; 1990–98 *World Development Report 1999/2000*, Table 11. Gross Domestic Product: 1950–73 and 1973–92, Maddison, Tables 3–15, 3–16, 3–17; 1990/98 *World Development Report 1999/2000*, Table 11.

live in a new era in which poor countries increasingly succeed in penetrating export markets with manufactured goods. This success has, in all likelihood, contributed to the rapid economic growth they are experiencing.

The importance of the developing world's increased educational attainment in facilitating its success in exporting manufactured goods to global markets is suggested by Table 2.4. In this table the same thirteen largest developing countries explored in Tables 2.1–2.3 are ranked by their level of merchandise exports per capita in 1998, a measure that indicates the degree to which a country is integrated into the world economy, with data also provided for each country's literacy rate in 1997. Here evidence of a positive association between per capita exports and literacy levels would support the hypothesis that a well-educated labor force is required for a country to participate successfully in the global economy. However, again the possibility of a reversal causality must be conceded. It might be that high export levels provided the countries with the resources to achieve high literacy rates.

TABLE 2.4. Exports per capita (1998) and adult literacy rates (1997) for selected large poor countries

Country	Merchandise Exports per Capita (Millions of $)	Adult Literacy Rates (Percent)
Mexico	1,224.01	90.1
Thailand	878.28	94.7
Turkey	414.92	83.2
Philippines	391.07	94.6
Brazil	307.08	84.0
Indonesia	239.41	85.0
China	148.31	82.9
Nigeria	85.62	59.5
Egypt	64.07	52.7
Pakistan	63.41	40.9
India	33.89	53.5
Bangladesh	29.98	38.9
Ethiopia	9.03	59.5

$r^2 = 0.699944$, significant at the 0.01 confidence level.
Source: Merchandise Exports Per Capita computed from the World Bank, *World Development Report 1999/2000* (New York: Oxford University Press, 2000), Tables 1 and 20. Adult Literacy Rates: United Nations Development Programme, *Human Development Report 1999* (New York: Oxford University Press, 1999), Table 10.

In any case, Table 2.4 reveals a positive, statistically significant linear relationship between exports per capita and literacy. Exports per capita tend to be higher in countries with high literacy rates than in countries where literacy is relatively low. Furthermore, no country with literacy under 80 percent experienced much success as an exporter. Exports per capita failed to reach $100 in each of the six nations with literacy rates below that level, while exports in the seven countries with relatively high literacy ranged from China's $148 to Mexico's $1,224.

Of course, other factors besides educational attainment influence export performance. Thus Thailand and the Philippines had nearly identical literacy rates, but the exports of the former were more than twice the level of those of the latter. Furthermore, as mentioned, a reverse causal flow was in all likelihood present as well. The income earned from exports may well have been used to fund advances in educational attainment. Nevertheless, what emerges from the table powerfully reinforces the view that a well-educated labor force is an important determinant of a country's success in becoming an exporter in the global economy.

The lesson in all of this is that globalization is not only about trade liberalization and technology. Abundant human capital too is necessary for a country to succeed in this process. Only when the modern technologies of communications, control, and information processing are joined with an educated labor force does participation in the global economy become feasible.

REDUCING POVERTY IN POOR NATIONS

Thus there is no doubt that the structure of the global economy has changed profoundly and that educational attainment has played an important role in this transformation. The question that arises, however, is what this change means for people's well-being. Globalization and economic development are not ends in themselves. They are desirable to the extent that they result in improved standards of living and, in particular, a reduction in poverty for the people who live in the countries experiencing these processes.

The problem is that a reliable time series by which to assess the direct relationship between globalization and poverty reduction does not exist. Information provided by the World Bank, for example, shows the percentage of the world's population living on less than $2.00 (U.S.) per day, certainly a level that should be thought of as impoverished. But these data are presented only in cross section, for one date, not over a period of years. The United Nations Development Programme does offer a human development index (HDI) and has provided this information for the years since 1975. But aside from the fact that the method behind the index has changed, causing problems when comparing one year with another, an additional difficulty is present in using the HDI in relation to economic growth. One of the principle components of the HDI is per capita income adjusted for purchasing power parity (United Nations Development Programme 1999, 127). But per capita income is simply another way of expressing national output, and thus the HDI is flawed when it comes to assessing the impact of economic growth on human welfare over time. Because they are not independent of each other, the two measures will move together, invalidating efforts to determine how one affects the other.

In the absence of adequate time series information, the role of globalization in reducing poverty can be inferred only by doing a cross-sectional analysis comparing the poverty levels in the more advanced of the developing countries with those in the less advanced. To gain insight into what probably will happen over time, we contrast poverty levels among our selected thirteen large poor countries. When this is done, the pattern stands out in bold relief. The data in Table 2.5 suggest that globalization is indeed instrumental in reducing poverty. In this analysis, I use a direct measure of poverty – the percentage of the population living with incomes of less than $2.00 (U.S.) per day, and I divide the countries into three groupings: a group of the more advanced among them, with per capita GNP levels between $6,240 and $8,120; a middle group with a range between $2,940 and $3,670; and the lowest ranking group, with levels of $1,650 and below.

TABLE 2.5. Gross national product (GNP) per capita (purchasing power parity [PPP] adjusted), exports per capita, and the percentage of the population earning $2.00 (U.S.) per day for selected large poor countries

Country	GNP per Capita (PPP Adjusted) (1997)	Exports per Capita (1998)	Percentage of Population below $2.00 (Various Survey Years)
Mexico	$8,120	$1,224	40.0
Thailand	6,590	878	23.5
Turkey	6,430	415	NA
Brazil	6,240	307	43.5
WEIGHTED MEAN	6,789	641	38.6
Philippines	3,670	391	64.5
China	3,570	148	57.8
Indonesia	3,450	239	58.7
Egypt	2,940	64	51.9
WEIGHTED MEAN	3,535	168	58.0
India	1,650	34	88.8
Pakistan	1,590	63	57.0
Bangladesh	1,050	30	NA
Nigeria	880	89	59.9
Ethiopia	510	9	89.0
WEIGHTED MEAN	1,477	40	82.9

Sources: GNP Per Capita and Percentage of Population Below $2.00, World Bank *World Development Report 1999/2000*, Tables 1 and 4.

As revealed in Table 2.5, the more developed of these countries both export more and have far less poverty than the less developed nations. The differences are dramatic. While more than 80 percent of the population of the poorest nations lives on $2.00 (U.S.) per day or less, that percentage is less than 40 percent in the more advanced nations. Similarly, exports are clearly associated with both more economic development and lower poverty levels when the middle group of these countries is compared with the group of countries with the highest per capita GNP. Development does appear to be associated with globalization, and the two in combination are associated with reduced poverty.

It is important to repeat that the poverty level employed here is the desperately low level of $2.00 (U.S.) per day and that, even so, almost two in five people are recorded as living below that threshold in countries such as Mexico, Thailand, Turkey, and Brazil. Clearly there is no cause for the advocates of globalization to engage in complacent self-congratulation. Much must yet be done to overcome deprivation. Nevertheless, the inference to be drawn from these cross-sectional data is clear. To the extent that the cross section portrays what happens over time, it indicates that globalization contributes to development and that, together, development and the integration of global markets have a substantial impact on poverty reduction.

THREE

The Sources of Opposition

For many Americans the opening of United States markets to imports represents a threat (Scheve and Slaughter 2001, 13–45). They believe that expanded trade, particularly with poor nations, results in job loss, downward pressure on wages, and the undermining of environmental protection. Through the 1970s these concerns remained largely muted. But in the 1980s, when imports as a percentage of this country's gross domestic product started to rise dramatically, opposition to trade increased[1] (Aaronson 2001, 3).

While the claim for a "race to the bottom" in environmental standards lacks empirical support (Dasgupta et al. 1995; Fredriksson and Millimet 2000; World Bank 2000), there is validity to the argument that trade with poor counties puts downward pressure on wages and employment in at least some industries in the United States. This is because for potentially mobile firms the supply of labor includes overseas workers. Open markets in

---

[1] Imports of manufactured goods as a percentage of GDP stood at 3.55% in 1970, 6.09% in 1980, 7.51% in 1990, and 10.34% in 1999 (Council of Economic Advisors 2001, Tables B-1 and B-104).

conjunction with the new technologies of globalization mean that an increasing number of United States workers do find themselves in competition with third world workers. The result is that it has become more difficult for this segment of the United States labor force to secure wage increases (Rodrik 1997, 16). Firms can resist demands for wage increases by threatening to move production and if pressed sufficiently might actually do so.

The paradoxical fact is that the job loss and dislocations that occur in this way are actually the sources of the benefits associated with increased international trade. Imports from poor counties allow a rich country like the United States to shift its resources to new industries that are beyond the productive capacity of the underdeveloped world. These high-productivity industries will retain their market competitiveness even though they pay relatively high wages. With the increased importance of the high-wage sector and the reduced role for industries that pay low wages, the overall wage structure will increase. At the same time, the wealthy nation can, through imports, continue to have access to and consume the output of the now relocated industries and at prices that are lower than if the goods were produced domestically.

This means that there is little to be gained for a country like the United States to try to compete with third world countries by protecting low-productivity, low-wage industries. Protecting poorly paid jobs is not a rational goal in a high-wage economy. The relocation and loss of jobs that pay poverty level wages are a means to increase the relative importance of high-end occupations. In this way, imports provide a vehicle by which to achieve the restructuring that is a central characteristic of a dynamic economy and an important source of increased living standards.

Of course, the word "restructuring" is cosmetic. It conceals the fact that the transitions it implies possess the potential for inflicting great injury as well as benefits. Principally, this damage is caused by the occupational shifts imposed upon workers who have lost their jobs. These difficulties are far from trivial, and their ame-lioration necessitates policy interventions. Support is needed to ensure that the occupational and geographic dislocations that restructuring dictates are accomplished with as little pain to workers as possible. Such support can take the form of wage insur-ance for workers who lose their jobs, portable health insurance, expansion of earned income tax credits, and adult education and job retraining.

If globalization is to be fair, then, an enhanced rather than a reduced role for government is required. Supportive public sector policies are needed to make certain that displaced workers do not become the innocent victims of the structural changes that result from globalization. As Dani Rodrik frequently emphasizes, "for trade to be a source of gains in terms of efficiency and growth for an economy, it has to be associated with some destruction of jobs and some distributional consequences." He continues, "you cannot have a strategy of expanding trade if you do not have a complementary strategy at home that involves strengthening insti-tutions of social insurance, education and training, and compen-sation" (Rodrik 1998, 89, 91). Furthermore, there is a presumptive case that the costs of such programs should come from the increased income that trade itself generates.

This need for a policy of domestic support for the victims of trade liberalization has not commanded the attention it should. In emphasizing the benefits of trade openness its advocates did not deal adequately with the downside of the process. In particular, they were not forthright about the fact that trade displaces workers and industries even as it results in the availability of more goods at lower prices and employment at higher wages than would be possible in the absence of international sales.

The reason for this neglect lies in the politics of those who have advanced trade expansion. Trade advocates have all but ignored the issue of justice, concentrating their attention instead on the task of mobilizing the support of potential exporters. Their assumption has been that the prospect of lucrative export markets is sufficient to build a pro-trade constituency powerful enough to achieve their goals. They have omitted from consideration the claims for assistance made by those whose interests are damaged by the process.

Destler and Balint describe this political strategy as having been "enormously successful." By both limiting their agenda and not strongly advocating support mechanisms, the trade lobbyists and policy makers "excluded most divisive broader questions of social policy [and] the process remained reasonably bipartisan" (Destler and Balint 1999, 7). That is, they avoided having to come to terms with the costs of the expanded government support that those questions would have raised. According to Destler and Balint, "over the years, executive and congressional leaders became quite adept at managing this system, . . . responding to pressures to restrict imports with militant efforts to expand exports" (Destler and Balint 1999, p. 7).

The outcome of this political strategy was enactment of an expanded trade agenda. In 1976 the United States granted poor countries partial access to its markets without requiring reciprocal trade concessions. This agreement, the Generalized System of Preferences (GSP), was followed in 1983 by the Caribbean Basin Initiative (CBI), an agreement that opened United States markets to a list of non-traditional exports from the countries of and those bordering on the Caribbean. Like the GSP, the CBI did not require trade concessions by the poor nations. Ten years later, Mexico was granted enhanced access to United States consumers with the North American Free Trade Agreement (NAFTA). In this case, tariff reductions and other obstacles to trade were removed by both nations.

But the fact that the trade agenda was successfully pursued at the same time as cutbacks in governmental services to the working poor were instituted left the proponents of liberal trade defenseless against the charge that their project was fundamentally unfair (Aaronson 2001, 3).[2] And it was this perception of unfairness that provided the context in which a coalition emerged between those who were themselves victims of increased international trade and those who were sympathetic to the victims' plight. That coalition, seeing trade as the enemy, became an important wing of the anti-globalization movement.

What made trade seem particularly unfair was not only that compensatory policies were neglected but also that the trade initiatives undertaken by the government frequently were formulated in response to specific corporate pressures. Policy makers were responsive to the interests of American exporters at the same time as they all but ignored the dislocations associated with the trade expansion they were encouraging. The corporate sector was thus the main beneficiary of governmental efforts, while individual victims were largely abandoned to their fate.

Odell and Eichengreen report that United States negotiators "expended great . . . energy in many bilateral fights with allied countries on behalf of particular industries." Among the industries benefiting from this kind of attention were citrus farmers in California and Florida, corn farmers, cattle ranchers, lumber producers, cigarette makers, airplane manufacturers, automakers, and steel producers. They write that "pound for pound, the semiconductor industry achieved the most impressive Washington trade leverage." According to these authors, this country's negotiating agenda "bore the clear fingerprints of a huge coalition of U.S. industries seeking better protection of intellectual property rights" (Odell and Eichengreen 1998, 202). The *New York Times* reported

---

[2] Federal social welfare expenditures as a percentage of GDP declined from 11.4% to 10.9% between 1980 and 1990 (U.S. Census Bureau 2000, Table 599, p. 378). In 2001, only about 35,000 workers received income support from trade adjustment assistance programs, a number far lower than those affected by increased imports (Chen, 2002).

that in return for congressional support for trade agreements, the Clinton administration offered favors to producers of steel, cars, wheat, lumber, cement, ball bearings, cellular telephones, civil aircraft, and apparel (as cited in Odell and Eichengreen 1998, n. 25). Odell and Eichengreen explain that "during the unseen drafting of the implementing bills, lobbyists for each of these sectors managed to insert new special provisions benefiting themselves" (Odell and Eichengreen 1998, 203).

The failure to take into account the costs as well as the benefits of trade liberalization was not simply unfair: it did not take long for this failure to become politically damaging to trade advocates. Though the positive economic effects of enhanced trade are substantial in the aggregate, they typically are both small and hidden as experienced by individual workers and consumers. At the same time, however, trade's negative disruptions are dramatic. People lose jobs and firms relocate or go bankrupt. Thus the political problem for those who advocate liberalized trade arises because, in general, the hurt done by trade to specific individuals is more obvious and is felt more deeply than the benefits received from trade by the rest of the population. This is all the more the case if the supports in place to soften trade's negative consequences are inadequate.

As a result, many legislators feared that they would have to face a much better mobilized constituency of opponents of trade liberalizing legislation than of proponents of trade. The strategy adopted by trade liberalizers almost certainly ensured this would happen, for the only group involved in lobbying on behalf of international trade was the exporters, easily tarred as a special interest.

THE TRADE OPPONENTS

It was the struggle against NAFTA in the early days of the Clinton administration, write Destler and Balint, that "brought together for the first time a coalition of activist organizations, including grassroots environmental groups (such as the Sierra Club), the Ross Perot third-party movement, right-wing voices (such as presidential aspirant Pat Buchanan) and Public Citizen, the activist organization founded by consumer champion Ralph Nader" (Destler and Balint 1999, 9–10). Even when joined by organized labor, however, the coalition failed to prevent NAFTA's passage in 1993.

What changed the political dynamic and gave renewed clout to the trade opponents was the culmination, in 1994, of the Uruguay Round and the establishment, in 1995, of the World Trade Organization (WTO). That organization, and in particular its dispute settlement mechanism, provided trade opponents with a halo of nationalism, allowing them to present themselves as defenders of the national interest. With the establishment of the WTO, it was possible for trade opponents to maintain that an anti-trade position was a needed antidote for a presumably weakened United States sovereignty.

The WTO was conceived not by the United States but, according to Sylvia Ostry, by "a coalition of middle powers, both developed and developing." Canada had formally proposed the creation of the WTO, a proposal endorsed by the European Union (EU). The motivation of these countries, Ostry writes, lay in their recognition "that the alternative to a rules-based system would be a power-based system and that, lacking power, they had the most to lose" (Ostry 1999, 172). The European Union in particular, Ostry believes, "became an active supporter of a new institution that could house a single, strong dispute settlement mechanism, out of growing concern about U.S. unilateralism" (Ostry 1999, 172).

In contrast to the anti-trade forces in the United States, who believed America was giving away too much with NAFTA, America's trading partners worried that NAFTA symbolized the exercise of disproportionate power by the United States. Their concern was that America would embark upon a series of bilateral trade agreements and in that way shape the global trading environment to its own advantage. In this perspective, NAFTA threatened to create an environment in which global trade would now be shaped by and conform to the interests of one country only – the United States. According to Eckes "concerned that the United States had embarked on a bilateral course . . . Europe relaxed its objections to new multilateral negotiations" (Eckes 1999, 100).

GATT rules concerning trade were adopted by the WTO as a single package. But in addition to further reductions in tariff levels, the Uruguay Round negotiations broke new ground in several areas, the most important of which was the creation of an enforceable trade dispute resolution process. That innovation became a lightning rod for the opponents of expanded international trade.

Previously, under the GATT, when a dispute settlement panel sent its recommendations to the GATT Council for approval, the proposed settlement had to be unanimously accepted to become binding. This unanimity rule all but stripped the GATT of enforcement power. The nation against which the panel ruled was able to exercise a veto over a proposed settlement. John H. Jackson, a leading authority on international trade law, writes that this ability to void the findings of dispute panels "was deemed to be the most significant defect in the GATT process" (Jackson 1998, 167). To correct this flaw, the veto power was removed in the WTO. In the new organization, a panel report has to be adopted unless there is a unanimous vote against it. No longer can one country block a settlement. In the new process, a country that fails to comply with the recommended settlement after exhausting the appeals procedure becomes liable for "compensatory measures." These are sanctions that the aggrieved nation can impose on the violator; the level of these sanctions can equal the damage that was experienced.

The kind of alarm that the new dispute settlement procedure generated among trade skeptics is represented in the work of

Alfred E. Eckes, Jr. By agreeing to these provisions, Eckes writes, United States trade negotiators "yielded effective sovereignty to an international commercial organization (the WTO)" (Eckes 1999, 103). He bemoans the fact that "powerful nations like the United States [can] no longer take unilateral action to enforce rights under trade agreements as they pertained to members of the WTO" (Eckes 1999, 102, 103).

But the argument that the United States, because of its adherence to the WTO, has ceded its sovereignty is a serious exaggeration. For the fact is that there is nothing the WTO actually can do to force the United States to change its laws. At most, if it were found to be in violation of WTO rules, the United States could be made subject to trade sanctions by the victimized nation.

This said, the fact remains that international rules regulating trade do in some respects impinge on domestic policies. What the WTO and its enforcement power represent is an acknowledgment that in an increasingly integrated world economy there have to be enforceable rules governing trade. Disagreements and disputes in international trade are inevitable, and because that is so, a procedure for their resolution is needed. This, in turn, requires that nations voluntarily comply with agreed-upon codes of behavior. The failure to do so would make it impossible to construct an equitable system of global economic trade. Enlightened self-interest, therefore, dictates adherence to a dispute settlement mechanism.

A more serious objection to the dispute settlement process than the issue of sovereignty involves how the process works. Here again, the damage is self-inflicted by trade proponents. WTO hearings are not open to the public, and there is no formal procedure by which NGOs can participate in the work of the dispute settlement panels. There is thus no way that unofficial, non-corporate, voices can make themselves heard. This serious flaw is present in many aspects of the work of the WTO. Ostry refers to this as the WTO's "democracy deficit," a deficit that has provided important fuel to trade opponents. The concern that WTO decision makers might be unresponsive to American interests is not nearly as compelling as the objection that WTO decisions are made in secret and with no public accountability (Ostry 1999, 182).

THE SEATTLE WTO MINISTERIAL MEETING

By 1997 the anti-trade coalition was powerful enough to block the Clinton administration's proposed renewal of fast-track trade authority, an outcome that Destler and Balint call "a debacle for the President and for trade liberalization" (Destler and Balint 1999, 11). The withdrawal of fast track is described in such strong terms because, without the promise of a straight up or down congressional vote on trade agreements, it is not possible for United States representatives to define with credibility the country's settlement terms in trade negotiations. The positions that negotiators adopt in trade talks, in the absence of fast track, are subject to revision by Congress. The failure of fast track brought to a temporary close the period of wholesale signing of trade agreements by the United States. United States trade representatives simply lack the authority to deliver an agreement.

Even as the opposition to trade liberalization grew, however, President Clinton, in his 1999 State of the Union address, proposed that the WTO Ministerial Meeting scheduled for December 1999 be used to launch a new round of trade negotiations. Bob Davis, in the *Wall Street Journal*, speculates that this proposal was prompted by the administration's desire to project a "post-impeachment agenda." Though protest demonstrations were expected, Seattle, Washington, was considered a favorable location for such a meeting since that city's economy had benefited from the exports of locally based firms such as Boeing, Microsoft, and Weyerhaeuser (Davis 1999, 1). No one in authority seriously expected that the demonstrators who went to Seattle vowing to shut down the WTO would be large enough in numbers and sufficiently militant to require the city to impose a twenty-four-hour curfew in the area near the convention center where the trade negotiators met. But this is what occurred. When the WTO negotiators failed to agree on an agenda for future negotiations, the demonstrators declared victory.

The Seattle Ministerial Meeting revealed not only the strength of the opponents of trade liberalization but also the absence of consensus among the WTO members themselves. Most observers agree that even without opposition in the Seattle streets, the trade talks would likely have failed (Schott 2000, 5). The year prior to the Seattle meeting had been contentious within the WTO. Most dramatically, the organization's member countries had been unable to agree on a new secretary-general, ultimately resolving the dispute by dividing the job between two individuals, each to serve half a term.

By the time of the Seattle talks, the divisions within the WTO were many and crosscutting. For examples, the United States and a number of underdeveloped countries were in agreement in wanting to dismantle the European Union's agricultural programs protecting farmers from third world imports. But on other issues the United States and the underdeveloped world were in conflict. Third world textile exporting nations were frustrated by the refusal of the United States to accelerate the pace at which its tariffs on imports of clothing were to be reduced. In another area, there was extensive support for a Japanese initiative that opposed United States anti-dumping laws, which were seen by many countries as disguised protectionism and, as reported in The *Wall Street Journal*, "loathed by governments around the world" (Cooper, Davis, and Hitt 1999, 4). In another case, the United States earned the unremitting opposition of poor nations, but not of the European Union, when it advocated studying the connection between labor rights and future trade agreements.

Both the demonstrators and the delegates agreed that, whatever its cause, the failure of the Seattle WTO meeting was a decisive setback for trade liberalization. Those who favored freeing trade were in despair; those who opposed liberalization could hardly contain their glee. For trade liberalizers, the failure of the WTO to agree to a new negotiating round and the strength shown by the demonstrators were, in the words of *The Economist,* "a disaster" (*Economist* 1999, 1). *The Economist's* gloom was matched by the near euphoria of *The Nation,* which editorialized, "Seattle was indeed a milestone for a new kind of politics. Splits between labor and environmentalists, young and old, were not merely forgotten, they were actively overcome" (*Nation* 1999, 2). William Greider, *The Nation's* national correspondent, wrote that even before Seattle he had assumed that the WTO was a "doomed institution" and that he now did not "expect this queer duck of pseudogovernance . . . to survive" (Greider 1999, 1).

TRADE LIBERALIZERS RECONSIDER

In the aftermath of Seattle the advocates of trade liberalization awakened to their political peril and increasingly came to recognize the flaw in their political strategy. Only after globalization had been tarred by the one-sidedness of its corporate-dominated agenda did they begin to emphasize domestic compensatory policies. C. Fred Bergsten, a former government trade official and now director of the prestigious Institute for International Economics (IIE), for example, criticized President Clinton's 1999 State of the Union address calling for fast-track trade negotiating authority. Bergsten complained that Clinton had failed to acknowledge explicitly that with trade liberalization "there are costs and that there will be losers" as well as winners. Instead of speaking of domestic policy separately from trade, the president "should have linked his domestic reforms and his trade liberalization, arguing that the former is the most constructive solution to the shortcomings of the latter." Bergsten argued that "the case for the United States to move ahead in the WTO is powerful . . . but we obviously must have the domestic components of the program to drive and support it" (Bergsten 1999, 199).

Others also came to a belated recognition of the need for domestic adjustment mechanisms. Destler and Balint, for example, urged that in the future an important element of a trade strategy "must be domestic policy measures that reinforce the social compact in the face of pressures from globalization and broader technological change" (Destler and Balint 1999, 1, 56). A Brookings Institution publication defending trade made the same point, noting that "a standard remedy for the economic fallout from free trade is to require that the winners share some of their gains with the losers through some form of compensation. We take this seriously as a political requirement and a moral obligation" (Burtless et al. 1998, 131–2).

Nevertheless, trade policy remains an issue about which the country is deeply divided. Enhanced trade-negotiating authority was passed by the House of Representatives in a 215–214 vote in December 2001. But as of this writing (June 2002), it remains uncertain that the Congress will, in granting this power, also adequately strengthen ameliorative programs that soften the dislocations associated with increased trade. Policy makers still do not sufficently appreciate that foreign economic and domestic social policies need to be linked. The result is that international trade opponents continue to retain the moral high ground with regard to the costs of increased international economic integration.

Trade policy thus remains a polarizing issue. The opponents of trade agreements remain formidable because the grievances of those injured by trade liberalization have gone unaddressed. But at the same time, the anti-globalists are not powerful enough to reverse a process that is deeply rooted in the power of new technology and also advances the interests of large numbers of people worldwide. The upshot is that when new trade agreements are negotiated and brought to the Congress a contentious battle will ensue, not only in the legislature but also in the country more generally. That battle will be the price paid for neglecting the domestic impact of international trade and failing to construct a consensus that promotes both an enhanced and a just process of globalization.

FOUR

Alternatives to Globalization

When in late 1997 the Clinton administration withdrew its request for fast-track authority, *The Nation* celebrated. It editorialized that "against overwhelming odds, a mobilization of labor unions, environmentalists, consumer and church groups managed to torpedo the centerpiece of the corporate trade agenda." But at the same time *The Nation* was eager to dispel the idea that the defeat of fast track signaled a retreat to narrow isolationism. Rather, it described the outcome as a triumph of a "new internationalism." The withdrawal of fast track, it wrote, represented a "call to put America's weight on the side of worker, consumer and environmental movements globally" (*Nation* 1997, 3). Two weeks later, the magazine's national correspondent, William Greider, reiterated this position. While applauding the defeat of fast track, he attacked "nostalgic, right-wing protectionists." Greider argued that "even if pulling up the bridges were a plausible course, it would be profoundly unprogressive." Echoing *The Nation* editorial, Greider insisted that it was important for Americans to "learn to think globally." He called on the people of the country to resist the temptation to try to "withdraw from the world" and to "think instead of grand new vistas that have been opened for human relations around the world" (Greider 1997, 12).

This call for a "new internationalism," however, does not stand unchallenged among anti-globalization activists. Within the movement an alternative perspective wants to turn away from the grand vistas envisioned by Greider. Instead, it celebrates the local. Movement activists who share this viewpoint believe that the geographic scale of production, investment, and distribution should be reduced from worldwide to smaller units. In this perspective, globalization is rejected in favor of greater self-reliance and community autonomy.

That this alternative is of significance among movement activists is attested to by Naomi Klein, herself a sympathetic observer of the anti-globalization movement. She writes that the localist perspective is gaining ground among activists and that "there is an emerging consensus that building community-based decision-making power . . . is essential to countering the might of multinational corporations" (Klein 2000, 2).

The conflict between localism and the kind of internationalism advocated by *The Nation* has not been acknowledged by the movement itself. Nevertheless, the clash between the two is fundamental. One attempts to shape globalization, the other hopes to abandon it. It is hard to see how the two can be reconciled. A major fault line therefore is present in the anti-globalization movement, threatening its solidarity.

The movement has been able to paper over this disagreement, however, by emphasizing what it opposes, not what it favors. Both wings see contemporary globalization as driven by and primarily beneficial to multinational corporations. Both seek to curb that dominance. Their disagreements therefore are not over a need to constrain the corporate sector. Rather, they disagree over whether the globalization process, whatever its form, should be scrapped.

There are, of course, big problems associated with the movement's inability to agree on the shape of what it would like to see constructed. If support from a wider segment of the population is to be attracted, it will be necessary for the anti-globalists to identify what they advocate as well as what they are against. In particular, it will be necessary to answer such questions as how multinational corporations are to be limited and what the consequences of such limitations will be. If they are eliminated, what if anything will replace them? These are important issues that will have to be satisfactorily resolved before the anti-globalists can legitimately claim that they deserve a serious role in shaping policy. But doing so will require that the movement come out either on one side or the other of its internal divide. At the moment there does not seem to be an inclination to face up to this choice.

Unfortunately, neither choice is attractive. Both the new internationalist and the localist positions fail to offer the kind of reform program that contemporary globalization requires. What is needed is a policy agenda that both preserves the development-promoting aspects of the process and, at the same time, reduces the damage the process inflicts on innocent victims. The problem is that neither of the two positions present in the movement is a likely source of such a creative synthesis.

As we will see, the movement's internationalism is, in effect, the advocacy of an undisguised exercise of United States unilateralism in shaping global labor and environmental standards. It would, as a consequence, almost certainly be resented by our trading partners and therefore be the source of trade-disrupting contention. The ensuing arguments and disagreements could well slow globalization, as well as result in a deadlock over the introduction of labor and environmental standards. The localists present a program that would have an even higher price tag associated with it. Their rejection of modernism would militate against further substantial increases in output and income. Since that in turn would foreclose the possibility of a widespread increase in living standards, this approach too is unsatisfactory.

INTERNATIONAL NATIONALISM

An important component of the anti-global movement believes that globalization can be made equitable only through the exercise of American power. It advocates the use of trade sanctions – the curtailing of trade with the United States – until such time as other nations conform to specified labor, human rights, and environmental standards. In this, there is an explicit endorsement of what Michael Lind calls "a straightforward American nationalism" (Lind 1995, 5). This position is echoed in Jeff Faux's defense of "a liberal economic nationalism" (Faux 1996, 201) and in James Fallows's defense of the "the Germanic view" of economics, which, in contrast to the Anglo-American emphasis on the individual, is "more concerned with the welfare – indeed sovereignty – of people in groups, in communities, in nations" (Fallows, 1997, 315).

Examples of this turn to nationalism with respect to trade are abundant. In a briefing paper that he prepared for the liberal Economic Policy Institute (EPI), Jerome Levinson is nothing if not candid. According to him, efforts to achieve labor rights through multilateral negotiations have "reached a dead end." As a result, Levinson concludes, the only way to secure such rights is to pursue a policy that "relies on unilateral action by the U.S. government with respect both to bilateral agreements and to its participation in international trade and finance agencies." In calling for "aggressive unilateral action," Levinson maintains that trade preferences and financial assistance should be granted to countries on the basis not of their level of development or geographic location but on whether they adhere to "core labor rights." He writes:

> U.S. trade law should be changed to require that the Secretary
> of Labor certify that a country's workers can exercise core

worker rights before the STR [special trade representative] can grant a trade preference. Without such certification, the Treasury could not instruct the executive directors in the IFIs [international financial institutions] to vote in favor of proposed financing for a particular country. (Levinson 1999, 4)

Jeff Faux, the president of the EPI, agrees. In a book intended to influence the policies advocated by the Democratic Party, Faux writes "Democrats should stand for denying access to U.S. markets to countries like China with no effective [labor] standards and for making such standards part of the criteria for international lending agencies" (Faux 1996, 200). Thomas Palley of the AFL-CIO goes even further. His position is that trade sanctions should be applied not only against countries that fail to endorse core labor rights but also against nations where low wages prevail. According to Palley, where "the only reason for trade is the low wage structure and absence of social overhead costs, then trade should be managed through imposition of a social tariff," that is, through a tax to "compensate for low wages and lack of commitment to social goals" (Palley 1998, 172).

What underlies this call to exercise unilateral power is the conviction that in the absence of United States–imposed labor standards, trade with poor countries will result in Americans' losing the gains in wages and working conditions they have fought to secure. These economic nationalists believe that only if and when the gap between wages paid in poor countries and those paid in the United States is narrowed will American worker interests be protected. Similar arguments are made for the environment and human rights. In general, this segment of activists is convinced that imports from poor nations, as well as investment in them by United States corporations, undermine well-being in this country. Greater parity in wages, in working conditions, and in environmental and human rights standards is needed before trade with such countries can be fair for workers in this country.

On its face, the argument that trade sanctions can be an effective tool in raising wages in poor countries would seem untenable. If exports from an underdeveloped country were curtailed in an effort to pressure it into adopting a higher wage structure, the immediate impact would more likely be in the opposite direction. A United States limit on imports in the name of enhancing labor rights almost certainly would result in job losses in the poor nation, a reduction that would undermine labor's power to organize and bargain collectively for higher wages. Paul Krugman's sarcasm is depressing but well targeted when he writes that "the cause that has finally awakened the long dormant American left is that of – yes! – denying opportunity to third-world workers" (Krugman 2000, 2).

But the argument for trade sanctions is not entirely refuted in this way. Its advocates contend that low wages in poor countries are not the consequence of economic processes, but the result of repressive governmental measures. When such repression prevails, they argue, trade with the United States should be barred. To do otherwise would be to reward tyranny. Thus in defending his view on setting conditions on trade, Faux insists that the causes of poverty and low wages are fundamentally political. He argues that labor standards are needed "to curb . . . regimes' ability to suppress wages and routinely beat, jail and even kill workers who protest" (Faux 1998, 82). Poverty in the underdeveloped world is caused by politics, and trade policy should be guided by that understanding. In this perspective, what the United States should do is use its economic power to induce policy changes in undemocratic regimes – governments that are unlikely to initiate reforms on their own and that are not responsive to the concerns of their populations. The only way that a reform such as the adoption of core labor standards will occur is if the United States insists on it and uses trade sanctions to penalize countries that do not adopt such standards.

The problem is that this political view of the origins of low wages in poor countries is almost certainly wrong. Stephen S. Golub has shown not only that countries with low wages also experience low levels of labor productivity but also that wages and productivity have tracked each other over time (Golub 1997, 11). When labor productivity rises, so do wages. Dani Rodrik's examination of this subject yields a similar conclusion. Though Rodrik's paper is entitled "Democracies Pay Higher Wages" he reports that 80 to 90 percent of the differences in wages among countries are explained by variances in productivity. The remainder he attributes to the presence of democratic institutions. According to Rodrik, if Mexico attained a level of democracy comparable to that in the United States, average wages would rise by only 10 to 30 percent and would still remain far below the United States level (Rodrik 1998, 1).

According to data provided by Golub, in 1993 wage rates in Mexico's textile industry stood at $2.93 per hour, compared to $11.61 per hour in the United States. That is, the hourly wage rate in Mexico was roughly 25 percent of the level in this country. Assuming that democracy were introduced to Mexico in the degree prevailing in the United States, Rodrik's work suggests that the hourly wage rate in the Mexican textile industry would rise to between $3.22 (with a 10 percent increase) and $3.81 (with a 30 percent increase). Mexican wages would increase to between 28 and 33 percent of the United States level. Though such an increase is not trivial, these calculations demonstrate that even if it were to be carried out, political reform in Mexico would not come close to closing the wage gap between that nation and the United States.

All of this points to the conclusion that wages are low in poor countries fundamentally because of underdevelopment, not political repression. Workers are willing to accept low wages in such nations because their employment options are limited. It therefore is all but certain that curtailing trade in order to reduce the gap in wages is doomed to fail. Shutting off or reducing trade with countries in which wages are low more likely will result in an increase in unemployment and downward pressure on wages than the reverse.

Even if oppression were an adequate explanation of low wages, the historical record gives little ground for optimism that a unilateralist United States would be an effective agent in advancing the interests of labor and environmentalists. Far from being a progressive agenda, United States policy on labor and environmental issues has tended to lag behind that of other developed countries. Thus, in a report prepared in July 1999, the International Confederation of Free Trade Unions (ICFTU) criticized the United States for not endorsing the International Labor Organization's (ILO) two core conventions on trade union rights, its two agreements on discrimination, and its convention on child labor and for endorsing only one of its two conventions on forced labor (International Confederation of Free Trade Unions 1999, 1–2). Furthermore, within the United States, less than 10 percent of the private sector labor force belongs to unions. Perhaps facetiously, Jagdish Bhagwati has asked whether the United States itself is in conformity with the labor standards that authors like Faux advocate (Bhagwati 1998, 58–59).

The same skepticism is in order concerning the appropriateness of assigning the enforcement of environmental standards or human rights exclusively to the United States. The United States is by far the world's leading producer of both hazardous waste and carbon dioxide emissions, the latter a greenhouse gas responsible, at least in part, for global climate change (United Nations Development Programme 1999, Tables 19 and 18). Most recently, the Bush administration announced that it would not adhere to the Kyoto Protocal on global climate change. And, as is true for the labor conventions, the United States is hardly a leader with regard to human rights agreements. It has failed to adopt or to ratify four of the eight covenants or conventions covering human rights that have been internationally accepted since 1951. The United States has still not ratified the 1966 International Covenant on Economic, Social and Cultural Rights, the 1989 Convention on the Rights of the Child, the 1979 Convention on Eliminating Discrimination against Women, and the 1951 Convention on the Status of Refugees (United Nations Development Programme, Table 29). Despite this record, analysts such as those working at the EPI would vest in the American government responsibility for enforcing environmental and human rights standards worldwide.

Under these circumstances it is hard to find a basis for concluding that economic nationalism is a viable strategy for reforming globalization. Since trade sanctions are promised if the wage gap is not closed and since it is all but certain that that gap can be only minimally reduced if at all in the foreseeable future, the most likely result were the economic nationalists to have their way would be a reduction in trade with the underdeveloped world. It is not surprising, therefore, that their proposals elicit a vehemently hostile reaction from the poor nation themselves. When, for example, President Clinton gave an interview at the Seattle Ministerial Meeting in which he endorsed the use of core labor standards and suggested that failure to comply should be punished by WTO sanctions, his statements, according to the coverage provided by the *Wall Street Journal*, "enraged trade ministers from developing countries. They contended that it confirmed their worst fears that the United States was looking for a way to impose high tariffs on their products and take away the comparative advantages they enjoy with lower wage scales" (Associated Press 1999, 3; Winestock 2000, 1).

Rather than accept the validity of this argument concerning the sources of comparative advantage in poor countries, or even try to refute it, the advocates of United States unilateralism too often simply attack those who make it. Robert L. Borosage is representative of these advocates when he writes that "WTO trade delegates from the developing world tend to be comfortable members of the global elite that make out well under the current global rules." Because their interests are not represented by their government, Borosage continues, workers from those countries "find themselves caught in the proverbial race to the bottom" (Borosage 2000, 20). Predictably, the conclusion drawn by Borosage is that multilateral negotiations are futile and that the United States either should curtail trade with poor countries or else set as a condition for such trade that the poor countries accept the labor and environmental standards that the United States insists upon.

Many of the goals sought by the trade nationalists are of course desirable. But there is little likelihood that the shortcut of a unilateral imposition by the United States is the way to achieve them. Trade wars and contraction in global commerce are more likely outcomes than the diffusion of democratic and environmentally supportive policies. Rather, the fundamental means to achieve the goals of increased wages and a higher standard of living is through economic growth. Indeed, support for trade sanctions is very nearly perverse in this regard. Enhanced market opportunities, not their curtailment, are necessary for the job creation that would advance labor's bargaining strength in poor nations. Moving in the opposite direction would slow growth and thereby weaken the ability of workers to secure increased wages and benefits.

That trade should not be held hostage to labor, environmental, or human rights agreements does not mean that there is no role for diplomacy in their attainment. Multilateral agreements in these areas are possible and can be secured without the complications of linking them to trade. Labor standards, for example, could be negotiated at the ILO, with violators subject to a schedule of ILO-imposed fines. Agreement would not be easy. Not only would there be the need to come to a consensus on standards, but the ILO's enforcement machinery would have to be greatly strengthened. For environmental issues, the United Nations Environment Program (UNEP) might be the best institutional context in which issues such as global warming could be debated. Illustrative of success with this approach are the recently concluded negotiations concerning changes in the United Nations Biosafety Protocol with regard to genetically modified foods. In this case there was agreement to permit countries to bar imports of any genetically altered seeds, microbes, animals, or crops that they considered to be a threat to their environment. This successful outcome was almost certainly because the problems raised by genetically altered seeds were discussed in isolation, detached from trade policy and the threat of trade sanctions (Pollack 2000, 1–2).

THE ANTI-GLOBALISTS

The other wing of the movement opposes globalization altogether. For them, the geographic scale of production, investment, and distribution should be reduced from global to smaller units. They see localism as the antidote to domination by multinational corporations.

The call for a "community-based economics" contained in the Green Party platform on which Ralph Nader ran for president illustrates this point of view. The platform advocates an agricultural system "that moves as rapidly as possible towards regional/bioregional self-reliance" and calls for support for enterprises engaged in local production and consumption. The platform explicitly opposes the North America Free Trade Area (NAFTA), the General Agreement on Tariffs and Trade (GATT), and the World Trade Organization (WTO) (Green Party Platform 2000, 26, 27, 31, 28).

This theme of support for localism was also adopted by a task force assembled by the International Forum on Globalization. The task force included the prominent activists Lori Wallach, Walden Bello, Helena Norberg-Hodge, John Cavanagh, Edward Goldsmith, Martin Khor, David Korten, and Jerry Mander. The group's draft document is quite explicit: it opposes "corporate-led economic globalization" because it "entails, first, and foremost, de-localization and disempowerment of communities and local economies." The group's position is that "[it is] necessary to reverse directions and create new rules and structures that consciously favor the local and follow the principle of subsidiarity, i.e., whatever activities can be undertaken locally should be" (International Forum on Globalization 1999, 3).

There are many difficulties with this viewpoint. While it is easy to demonstrate that foreign direct investment has an important role to play in economic development and that development permits poverty reduction, there is virtually no track record of success with which to defend localization as a strategy for reducing poverty. Studies by the World Bank consistently show that countries classified as "strongly inward oriented" in their development strategies experienced lower growth rates than did comparable nations that participated more in global markets (World Bank 1987, 78–94). From within the movement, Greider comes close to acknowledging this. He writes that the challenge is to define "plausible strategies and reasonable safeguards that enable a nation to concentrate first on inward-led development, *without losing access to capital markets*" (my emphasis; Greider 2000, 15). De-coupling and disengagement from the world economy have been attempted by a number of third world countries over the years. But in no case have economic modernization and rising standards of living been the outcome, and a large majority of these countries have abandoned the effort in favor of greater global economic integration (for the English-speaking Caribbean, see Mandle 1996, 95–124).

The fundamental difficulty with the localist point of view is that its advocates seem blind to its costs. Localism bars firms from taking advantage of the cost-reducing characteristics of advanced technologies in international communications, control, and transportation. The efficiencies achieved when large multinational firms participate in international trade and global production networks are lost. In favoring relatively small firms that are confined to local markets, the advocates of localization are choosing to confine production to lower amounts of a smaller range of goods at higher prices than would be the case in a globally integrated economy. The upshot is a diminution in international living standards. Because localization involves abandoning an important mechanism of contemporary economic development, there can be little doubt that it puts downward pressure on the well-being of the poor both in wealthy nations and in the underdeveloped world. This might be acceptable for the affluent, who are motivated by concerns other than escaping deprivation. But it certainly fails the global poor and their search for an improved standard of living.

Because localization cannot promise to raise standards of well-being, the best that a movement that endorses it can hope for is to have political nuisance value. There exists enough hostility to multinational corporations to fuel disruptive demonstrations. But in a world in which poor people everywhere hope for increased income, localization will not be able to mobilize large enough numbers to represent an important political threat to globalization. That localism offers very little hope for the poor to achieve a materially advanced way of life probably dooms it as a viable alternative to globalization.

A more stable and more just globalization is what the poor need. Neither the attempt to impose global standards by the United

States nor the wholesale rejection of modernization is the way to achieve that objective. A politics committed to these goals awaits political marginality. American nationalism puts global trade at risk, and localism denigrates the accomplishments associated with economic development. Neither, therefore, is likely to gain the adherence of the numbers necessary for its adoption.

FIVE

The Anti-Globalization Movement and the Multilateral Agreement on Investment

The anti-globalization movement claimed a great victory when, at the end of 1998, negotiations among the twenty-nine member countries of the Organisation for Economic Co-operation and Development (OECD) to secure an agreement to be known as the Multilateral Agreement on Investment (MAI) were abandoned. The MAI would have established rules defining and limiting the policies a host government could impose on direct foreign investment (Graham 2000, 2). The proposed agreement had become a priority concern for anti-globalists in April 1997 when, as Lori Wallach and Ralph Nader write, "a coalition of international citizens' groups managed to liberate a draft, text and had it posted on the internet" (Barlow and Clarke 1998, x). This coalition was composed of many of the same groups that had unsuccessfully opposed NAFTA in 1993 and had successfully fought fast-track legislation for trade agreements in 1998. Prior to the posting of the MAI draft, the OECD negotiations had gone on for two years, largely without attracting public attention. Thus Destler and Balint write of the "the astonishment of its drafters" that the MAI had become "the target of a virulent campaign by an Internet-linked coalition of NGOs, with Public Citizen and a group called the

Preamble Center playing lead roles" (Destler and Balint 1999, 35, 34).

THE MAI AND THE OPPOSITION

If the MAI text had been agreed to, signatory countries would have been bound by four fundamental principles. First, there was to be no discrimination in the treatment of foreign investors, as compared either to domestic investors or to investors from other countries party to the agreement. "National treatment" and the extension of "most favored nation" privileges were at the core of the proposed agreement (OECD 1998, 13). Second, there was to be a ban on the imposition of performance tests on foreign investors. The draft agreement enumerated twelve categories of requirements that were to be disallowed. Among these, a host country could not require a foreign firm to be an exporter, to use domestically supplied inputs, to transfer technology, to locate its headquarters in the host country, to achieve specified production targets, to meet a hiring quota, to establish a joint venture with local firms, or to achieve a minimum level of local equity participation (OECD 1998, 18–19). Third, there was a dispute resolution provision that allowed a firm to take a country before either a domestic court or an international arbitrator in pursuit of a claim that trading rules had been violated (OECD 1998, 58–71). Fourth, there was an investment protection clause that, among other stipulations, barred expropriation or nationalization without compensation (OECD 1998, 52–57).

Especially among American anti-globalists, the opposition to the MAI framed its position in the language of aggrieved nationalism. Present is an almost unremitting tone of hostility, bordering on chauvinism, to foreign investment. No reasoned explanation is offered for the implied suggestion that investment and managerial decisions made by corporations based in the

United States are superior to those of foreign firms. In opposing the proposed treaty the movement revealed a willingness to employ a language of xenophobia inconsistent with its claim to represent a new internationalism. There were good reasons to be against the MAI, but the nationalist rhetoric used by anti-globalists tended to cloud and distort the issues in favor of a too simple opposition to businesses based in countries other than the United States.

A pamphlet by Maude Barlow and Tony Clarke, *The Multilateral Agreement on Investment and the Threat to American Freedom*, endorsed by Wallach and Nader, illustrates this problem. Barlow and Clarke contend that "the MAI is bound to intensify the assault on U.S. economic sovereignty." This will occur because large European and Japanese firms "are well positioned to take full advantage of the MAI tools to gain a strong presence in the U.S. market and influence over policy development" (Barlow and Clarke 1998, 11–12). Under the MAI "unelected and unaccountable foreign-based corporations would be well equipped to manipulate the policies and directions of nation-states like the U.S" (22), and as a result, the tools the treaty gives them "pose a fundamental threat to both the sovereignty and democracy of American citizens" (23). In the chapter "Losing Economic Sovereignty," Barlow and Clarke report that in "forbidding governments to restrict ownership of certain kinds of real estate, industries, and businesses to state or U.S. residents, the MAI exposes the American economy to outside corporate influence" (55), and on the same page, they worry that the MAI, in conjunction with WTO rules on financial services, will likely "open the U.S. market further to foreign-owned banks, strengthening the role they play in the country's economy" (55). In Chapter 8, "Promoting Foreign Takeovers," the authors express their concern that "some key sectors of America's economy and society could be vulnerable to foreign takeover" (66) and fret that the rules concerning privatization "would leave public assets and public services totally vulnerable to foreign takeover" (67). This chapter contains alarms that European and Japanese corporations might take over the water supply system, the financial services sector (69–70), even the education system in the United States if that system were to be privatized (68). Similarly, the authors report that "foreign corporations may begin to have a hand in determining food quality standards in the United States" (70) and that MAI rules "could also be used by domestic companies to trigger increased foreign influence and control" when they form joint ventures with foreign-based corporations (71). Chapter 8 concludes with a warning: "in other words, the MAI serves to strengthen the hands of absentee landlords in the new global economy" (71).

Barlow and Clarke's pamphlet is not a reasoned discussion of the excesses involved in the proposed MAI clauses banning performance tests, establishing dispute resolution procedures, or barring expropriation or nationalization. It is instead an attack on "national treatment" of overseas businesses and on foreign investors in general. Repeatedly the language of the text suggests that foreign firms put the United States at risk. Foreign direct investment (FDI) is seen simply as a threat. The authors do not analyze either the issues in or the desirability of treating foreign investment in the same way as domestic investment (national treatment) and investment by other countries (most favored nation treatment).

Barlow and Clarke maintain that defeating the MAI "does not mean there should never be a global investment treaty. On the contrary, there may well be a real need for an agreement, especially given the expanding size and scope of transnational corporations and the recent exponential growth in worldwide investment" (91). But an examination of the ten-point "Citizen's Charter" that they offer as an alternative to the MAI suggests that they sought to limit, rather than promote, FDI and in the process constrain international trade. Only one of their ten points is at all concerned with the international economy, and that one does not explicitly discuss FDI. The other nine content themselves with general descriptions of desirable domestic objectives in social and economic areas, including employment, social programs, education, natural resources, small farms, taxation, the relation between financial interests and lobbyists and politicians, discrimination, and freedom of the press.

The only point of the charter that deals with global economics says, in its entirety: "implement a fair trade policy that preserves the capacity to meet national priorities for food, energy, technology, and other vital national resources and thereby reduce dependence on export-oriented development" (94). It is hard to read the last phrase in any way other than as an explicit rejection of global economic integration. It is a call to curb, not expand, international trade.

This kind of opposition to the MAI, then, is rooted in something other than a simple objection to the content of the proposed treaty. What seems to be at work here is the use of the MAI to make the case more generally against globalization. That ultimate objective may explain the rhetorical excesses in Barlow and Clarke's work. Thus the fact that the critique of the treaty itself is unconvincing may not really be relevant. The target may have been the larger universe of global economic integration of which the MAI was to be only a single component.

As we shall see, there are grounds for believing that the MAI's design was flawed. But an attack on foreign businesses in particular and on globalization more generally does not clarify the reasons why the MAI may have been a bad idea whose prospects for implementation were never very good.

DEEP AND SHALLOW INTEGRATION

The world of trade created by the GATT negotiations was a world of "shallow integration." Trade expansion was an important objective for policy makers; nevertheless, they preserved "national sovereignty over domestic policies" (Lawrence, Bressand, and Ito 1996, 1). Tariffs were dramatically reduced, and a general understanding was reached that countries would grant extensive access to their markets. But beyond this consensus, particularly before the Uruguay Round of trade talks during the late 1980s and early 1990s, there was very little effort to remove impediments to trade caused by internal policies and institutions. That would have required deep integration, a process of cross-border policy harmonization that was not on the negotiating agenda.

Confining trade liberalization to tariff reductions and avoiding deep integration are consistent with standard international trade theory. That theory teaches that the expansion of trade does not require policy harmonization among nations. Indeed, the argument is that differences in economic policies and institutions, as well as in natural resources and in the availability of inputs such as skilled labor and capital, are precisely the reason there is trade. Because of these differences, production costs are not identical. Economic theory assumes these variations. It then suggests that countries specialize in those industries in which they find they possess a relative cost advantage and that they use the income that is thereby earned to buy the products they want but cannot produce efficiently. With each country specializing, global output will be maximized, permitting a higher standard of living worldwide than if countries tried to attain self-sufficiency. As Lawrence writes, in this framework "different national practices that *affect* trade should be tolerated, as long as actors operating within each economy are granted national treatment and not discriminated against and/or as long as they do not cause injury to other nations" (emphasis is original; Lawrence 1997, 54–55).

The problem is that to a large extent events have overtaken the view that only tariffs can act as significant barriers to imports and that their reduction is all that is required to promote international trade. What calls the "shallow integration" of the GATT process into question are the technological changes that have facilitated overseas investment in productive facilities. Specifically, advances in information technology have made it increasingly feasible for multinational corporations to disperse their production activities in order to minimize their production costs (Dunning 1997, 12–38; James 1999, 65). They have been able to do this by establishing directly owned subsidiaries overseas or by purchasing intermediate goods from other firms. According to the United Nations Conference on Trade and Development (UNCTAD), in 1998 sales of this kind accounted for about two-thirds of world trade (United Nations 1999, 14).

In international production chains then, investment is undertaken to produce intermediate goods. What is occurring is, to be sure, the importing or exporting of goods. But those imports or exports occur only because the company involved or its licensee has made prior investments in production facilities in both countries. Thus policies concerned with attracting foreign investment have become policies that influence international trade as well. Those policies that impede investment have become in effect obstacles to exports and, as such, barriers to trade (United Nations 1999, 3–17). In turn that has meant a diminution in the efficacy of the GATT process, a process that focused primarily on reducing tariffs and was little concerned with what have come to be called non-tariff barriers to trade. The new pattern of geographically dispersed production means that there is no way that a consideration of imports and exports can be dissociated from an analysis of the incentives and requirements imposed on foreign investors. Trade is at least in part determined by investment policy.

The same kind of relationship between investment and globalization occurs in the service sector. Services are not tangible, and so production chains are not the issue. Instead, the issue of non-tariff barriers to trade emerges because for a firm to provide a service overseas it frequently must establish a physical presence, that is, it must engage in FDI. As a result, in sectors such as finance and communications, if international sales are to occur it is not the product that must be mobile, but the firm that must extend itself across borders.

The ability to disperse production geographically and the spread of the service sector internationally have resulted in a phenomenal increase in the flow of FDI across borders in recent years, especially in the developing countries. According to data compiled by UNCTAD, FDI inflows globally grew by an average rate of 24.3 percent between 1986 and 1990, 19.6 percent between 1991 and 1995, and 25.7 percent between 1996 and 1998. These rapid rates of increase meant that, in contrast to the situation that prevailed at the end of the 1980s, when the stock of FDI in place was negligible, by 1998 the value of FDI investment stood at a record $644 billion (United Nations 1999, 9). Just as important as these global flows was the fact that while between 1987 and 1997 FDI as a percentage of GDP grew by 40.9 percent among the high-income countries, in low- and middle-income countries that same statistic increased by 300 percent. The flow of foreign investment was particularly dramatic in East Asia and Latin America, but all regions of the third world experienced substantial increases (Table 5.1).

Though fundamentally driven by the new technologies in communications and control, and by reductions in transportation costs, the increase in FDI was also affected by policy changes. In recent years virtually all countries have stepped up their efforts to

TABLE 5.1. Gross foreign direct investment as percentage of gross domestic product,[a] 1987, 1997

	1987	1997	Percentage Change
World	1.5	2.4	60.0
High-Income	2.2	3.1	40.9
Low- and Middle- Income	0.3	1.2	300.0
East Asia and Pacific	0.3	1.2	300.0
Europe and Central Asia	0.0	1.2	–
Latin America and Caribbean	0.4	2.0	400.0
Middle East and North Africa	0.4	0.9	125.0
South Asia	0.0	0.2	–
Sub-Saharan Africa	0.4	1.0	150.0

[a] Purchasing power parity adjusted.
Source: World Bank, World Development Indicators, 1999, Table 6.1.

attract such investment. UNCTAD counted 145 changes in FDI regulatory policies made by sixty countries in 1998 alone, 94 percent of which were intended to create a more welcoming environment. This continues a trend started in the 1980s in which, as UNCTAD has put it, "most countries in all regions that until then had maintained widespread restrictions and controls on FDI undertook substantial revisions in the investment regimes, [engaging in] an unprecedented process of liberalization of previous FDI impediments" (United Nations 1999, 115). In this, many countries are following the lead of the nations belonging to the OECD. As that organization approvingly reports, "In many cases there are

now few or no special approval procedures. Foreign-firm investment is treated in the same way as that of domestic firms, with
equal access to general incentives" (OECD 1996, 61).

The greatly enhanced relationship between investment and
trade has produced pressures to deepen global economic integration. Investment policies in an earlier era were left to the dis-
cretion of individual countries and became a determinant of each
nation's comparative advantage. But to facilitate cross-border
investment flows, countries increasingly have agreed to harmonize
their treatment of foreign investors. An important element in this
shift has been the negotiating of bilateral investment agreements
between countries with close economic relations. In 1997 alone,
108 such bilateral investment agreements were signed, bringing
the total number of these investment-facilitating accords to 1,726
(United Nations 1999, 117). In these pacts, the general direction
is to encourage and facilitate FDI and to accede to the needs and
preferences of the investors. These compacts mean that, increasingly, national autonomy in investment policies has become attenuated as countries agree to make their approach to FDI consistent
with that of their trading partners. If at one time it was possible
to attain "the acknowledged collective benefits of freer trade
and integrated global markets . . . while sacrificing a minimum of
national sovereignty" (McCulloch 1990, 542), it is now clear that
that trade-off has been altered in favor of deeper integration. The
growth in FDI has moved trade policies beyond external tariffs.
Countries have harmonized investment policies in order to participate in the global economy and, in the process, have conceded
some of their autonomy in economic policy making.

The movement to harmonization was felt in multilateral contexts as well as in bilateral relations between nations. According
to Frieder Roessler, the former director of the Legal Affairs
Division of GATT, "the pressure to negotiate rules on domestic
policies in the GATT rounds of trade negotiations" increased with

the passage of time. The first efforts in this regard were made as early as the 1973–79 Tokyo Round and resulted in an agreement on the content of technical regulations. Roessler writes, "As the Uruguay Round came to a close . . . new demands for bringing domestic policy matters into the multilateral trade order were made" (Roessler 1996, 21, 22, 42). Even so, the Uruguay Round resulted only in one agreement, the Agreement on Trade-Related Aspects of Intellectual Property Rights (TRIPs), that actually required each signatory to meet minimum standards of compliance, a defining element of deep integration. The Agreement on Trade-Related Investment Measures (TRIMs) was also achieved in the Uruguay talks, but its scope was limited. Krueger writes that TRIMs "did not cover many of the more general issues governing investment in one country by nationals of another" (Krueger 1998, 408). Brewer and Young agree, pointing out that the significance of these agreements resided less in their actual content than in the fact that "they establish[ed] investment issues on the WTO agenda for the indefinite future" (Brewer and Young 1996, 20, 10).

At the time of its signing in 1993, the NAFTA agreement among Canada, the United States, and Mexico represented a high-water mark for deep integration. Fundamentally an agreement to facilitate trade, NAFTA did so, in part, by harmonizing the investment policies of the three signatories. But the agreement covered only Canada, Mexico, and the United States. At most, therefore, NAFTA was only a model of what might be accomplished globally (Brewer and Young 1996, 20, 11).

THE FAILURE OF THE MAI

The MAI was the most ambitious effort to achieve agreement on the rules governing FDI. Arguing that "foreign direct investment is key to achieving" rapid growth globally, Donald J. Johnston, secretary-general of the OECD, championed the MAI negotiations.

According to his argument, "Nations have been well-served by commonly accepted rules for international trade. It is time to agree on multilateral rules for international investment" (Johnston, 1997, 2). Like the bilateral investment agreements and NAFTA, the MAI would have ensured that investors encountered identical governmental policies, in this case in all twenty-nine of the most developed countries in the world – the members of the OECD – not just in a handful of them. In general, as Alan P. Larson, a member of the United States negotiating team put it, the objective of the MAI talks was "to develop stronger disciplines and stronger protection for foreign investors in some new areas" (Larson 1997, 2).

According to William H. Witherell, the OECD's director for financial, fiscal and enterprise affairs, the need for the MAI stemmed from the limitations in existing agreements such as the TRIMs, which meant that "foreign investors still encounter investment barriers, discriminatory treatment and legal and regulatory uncertainties." Investors were "calling for a more secure, straightforward and consistent framework in which to conduct their international operations" (Witherell 1995, 3, 5). Witherell also pointed to the shortcomings of having a multiplicity of bilateral investment agreements. He warned of "a danger of spreading individualistic or self-centered solutions (either bilateral or regional) and conflicting rules." In this piecemeal approach lurked the danger of inconsistencies among the bilateral agreements, as well as ambiguities concerning the treatment of non-signatories. Thus it was, as Witherell reported, that "investment-policy makers and international business circles" perceived "the need for something more: a comprehensive framework of binding investment rules which is sufficient to meet the requirements of the new international investment environment" (Witherell 1995, 6, 3, 5). In a letter to the editor of the *Financial Times*, the OECD's Donald J. Johnston wrote that "predictable and transparent laws and regulations offer the prospect of greater investment flows, lower risk premiums and higher returns to investors" (Johnston 1998, 1).

The problem is that the larger the group of countries involved in negotiating an agreement such as the MAI, the less likely it is that their efforts will meet with success. Thus "its worldwide scope makes the WTO an attractive forum for worldwide harmonization efforts . . . but the range of policies for which worldwide harmonization is desirable and attainable is likely to be very small" (Roessler 1996, 42). At the same time, however, if negotiations were undertaken in a more narrow grouping, in which the chances of successfully concluding an agreement were enhanced, other kinds of problems would emerge. After the twenty-nine-member OECD initiated talks on the MAI, Krueger wrote that "the relationship of the developing countries to this code was a major concern." Her anxiety was that in such an approach "developing countries would naturally feel left out and be unlikely to embrace it" (Krueger 1998, 408). However, Krueger's concern was probably misplaced. A successfully negotiated MAI by the OECD members would almost certainly have compelled the compliance of virtually all the remaining trading countries, even though most of them were not party to the negotiations. Its failure to sign the treaty might well have meant a country would be shunned as a destination for FDI. Its failure to adhere to the treaty would have cast a cloud over a country's investment climate.

Talks started in May 1995, and the original idea was that the MAI would be completed in two years. But the difficulty of the negotiations forced the deadline back a year, until May 1998. By the beginning of that year, it was clear that hopes for a comprehensive treaty were receding. Guy de Jonquieres, a columnist for the *Financial Times*, reported that "one by one, most of the grand objectives set for the negotiations . . . have been dropped" (de Jonquieres 1998, 2). In February 1998, the United States representatives conceded that it was not possible to conclude the agreement on time. In October 1998 further talks were suspended, and when in December 1998 the French withdrew from the negotiations, the MAI was officially declared dead.

What made the negotiations difficult and ultimately end in failure was that countries that were quick to demand harmonization on issues where policy coordination either gave them an advantage or was consistent with their preferences were the same nations that demanded exceptions and the right to preserve policy differences where coordination would not benefit them. The contradictory position of the United States illustrates the point. Stuart Eizenstat, one of the United States officials most closely involved in the negotiations, reported that this country was particularly concerned about "ambiguous and non-transparent carve-outs [exceptions]" that the countries belonging to the European Union were demanding for all EU members. That position, argued Eizenstat, "strikes at the core of the non-discrimination principle fundamental to the MAI." As an example, he objected to "an overly broad carve-out for culture," maintaining that it "would leave a large hole in the agreement in areas of commercial importance to U.S. firms, such as telecommunications and computer software" (Eizenstat and Lang 1998, 2). In addition, the United States objected to proposals that would exempt film, radio, and television from provisions of the agreement.

But even as the United States was complaining about the exceptions demanded by others, Secretary Larson reported that the United States was concerned that the agreement not impede its own regulatory activities in the areas of health, safety, and the environment. Furthermore, he expressed his country's anxiety that the treaty did not yet contain language that would adequately safeguard those regulations and protections that had been adopted at the state and local levels. Support for racial minorities in the United States was another area of potential conflict with the MAI. Secretary Larson was also intent on protecting the ability of United

States governmental agencies to favor American firms. He reported that he had "proposed U.S. exceptions for subsidies and government procurement; these would protect future as well as existing programs which discriminate against foreign investors" (Larson 1998, 2–3).

Not only the United States but virtually all of the participating nations made claims for exceptions. Lawrence had foreseen at least part of the problem when he wrote that "the difficult task [in negotiating the MAI] would be to determine those issues on which harmonization would be essential and those in which differences must be tolerated" (Lawrence 1997, 66). With that being the case there was no surprise in the *Financial Times* report, in February 1998, that "even if a deal is struck, it is expected to do little more than codify OECD members' existing investor protection policies. The MAI will essentially ratify the status quo, says one negotiator" (de Jonquieres 1998, 2). In the end, of course, not even that was achieved, as negotiations broke off in failure.

A VICTORY FOR THE MOVEMENT?

The NGOs in opposition to the MAI celebrated when negotiations for the agreement terminated. Public Citizen declared that the MAI failure "was an exciting victory that proved that citizen activism can still beat the transnational corporate agenda" (Public Citizen n.d., 1), and the Preamble Center spoke of a "significant victory" (Preamble Center 1998, 1).

Their claims of triumph, however, may overstate the anti-globalists' role in the failure of the MAI. Even if NGO pressure had not been present, the MAI talks probably would not have suceeded. It is far from certain that the dispensations that participating countries were calling for in defense of their industries, institutions, and values could have been satisfactorily reconciled with the underlying principles of the proposed agreement. A disappointed supporter of the MAI, Edward M. Graham, put it this way: "one might compare the MAI in its last few months to a ship that is taking on water and is in distress but has not yet foundered. The NGOs torpedoes, in this analogy, sealed the ship's doom, but one will likely never know whether, were it not for the torpedoes, the ship might have eventually reached a safe harbor" (Graham 2000, 16).

Even if agreement had been reached, the MAI's next hurdle would have been at least as difficult as the negotiations themselves. Congressional approval would not have been easy since opposition would have appeared on both the political right and the political left. In all likelihood the MAI's provisions would have generated a nationalist opposition among conservatives, an opposition sufficiently similar to the position taken by anti-global activists on the left to encourage both sides to join in coalition (Lizza 2000, 23–25).

In responding to the MAI the anti-globalists put their hostility to the Helms-Burton Act in abeyance, suggesting that hope for such a coalition was not illusory. Helms-Burton calls on the United States to impose sanctions unilaterally on firms that invest in Cuba. It, however, has generated a great deal of opposition both internationally and domestically. Numerous nations have objected to the extension of United States government authority to business decisions made by foreign firms in international markets. At home, Helms-Burton has been opposed, especially by liberals, as an unfair imposition on a small country.

Nevertheless, Barlow and Clarke joined Republican members of Congress in opposing the efforts of negotiators representing Canada and the European Union to ban from the MAI the kind of secondary boycotts that Helms-Burton envisioned (Destler and Balint 1999, 34). Though Barlow and Clarke acknowledged that it was "a complicated issue for legislators and human rights groups in North America," they nevertheless came down on the side of

Helms-Burton, arguing that if the act's provisions were banned "government will no longer have the capacity to use investment sanctions to influence human rights (and environmental) practices around the world" (Barlow and Clarke 1998, 79). For both the anti-global movement and the political right, the ability of the United States to exercise its power was more important than the establishment of universal rules that in governing trade would constrain such unilateralism.

Much more of this kind of opposition would have emerged had the treaty successfully been negotiated. For, fundamentally, considerable overlap exists between the "new internationalist" left and the political right in defense of the exercise of unilateral power by the United States. To be sure, the ends sought by the two camps in the use of such power differ. Nevertheless, each group is committed to preserving United States autonomy in both domestic and international affairs. In coalition against the MAI, they would have represented a formidable bloc that might have prevented a negotiated MAI from securing congressional approval.

TOP DOWN OR BOTTOM UP?

The MAI never came to a Senate vote. The effort within the OECD represented an overreach. It called for a degree of harmonization and diminution of sovereignty involving investment policies that went beyond what could be attained. But that the MAI failed does not bring the matter to a close. To begin with, multinational corporations are politically powerful and have a vested interest in a liberal regime with regard to investment. They almost certainly will continue to pressure governments about harmonizing investment rules and securing some kind of investment agreement. Moreover, beyond the issue of power remains the fact that obstacles to investment act as barriers to trade and thus as barriers to benefits that new technologies make possible. Societies are better off economically when FDI mobility is at a high level. Because this is so, the issues raised by the MAI were not resolved by the MAI's demise. Indeed, the groups among the anti-globalists recognized this, warning their memberships that their success with regard to the MAI might prove to be short-lived. Even as it congratulated the movement for its victory, Public Citizen pointed out, "Yet before champagne could be chilled to celebrate the MAI's demise, its corporate and governmental supporters were seeking to revive the MAI's agenda" (Public Citizen n.d., 2).

It is hard to envision how the anti-globalization forces can prevail over the long term in opposing FDI mobility. Virtually all nations have an interest in attracting investment, notwithstanding the fact that they simultaneously would like to preserve as much national policy autonomy as possible. The poor countries need and want to attract FDI to develop; the economically advanced countries support mobility in the name of the multinational corporations located in their countries and because trade generally allows their economies to grow and become more efficient. Neither the "Citizens' Charter" drafted by Barlow and Clarke nor anything like it can become the basis of future trade negotiations. That document simply does not adequately address the issue of how to manage the international economy.

At the same time, the MAI failure identified the probable limits of contemporary global integration. It demanded a ceding of autonomy in policy making that was politically unrealistic. Clearly, a scaling down from the requirements of the MAI is called for. Nevertheless, the case for a codification of global investment rules remains strong. What is needed is a rethinking of the MAI approach with a view to moving in the direction of its goals of non-discrimination and national treatment of foreign investment but, in so doing, respecting the limits of what is possible.

One approach to this rethinking would be to reduce the number of countries involved in investment talks. The model of NAFTA suggests itself, where three countries – two developed, one rela-tively underdeveloped – were able to finesse their conflicts and write a comprehensive trade and investment treaty. The fact is that this strategy has already been widely adopted. With NAFTA the prototype, bilateral investment treaties have proliferated in recent years. However, dissatisfaction with them is what gave rise to the MAI in the first place. For while such agreements do facilitate capital flows among the signatories, they do not extend to other countries. The patchwork pattern that thus emerges increases capital mobility, but nothing like universal mobility is secured.

Under the circumstances, it might be possible to successfully conclude a scaled-down agreement. A stripped down, less invasive investment treaty might secure a wide consensus. In the jargon of trade diplomacy, what this probably means is that the concept of a "top-down" agreement, as represented by the MAI, will have to be given up in favor of a "bottom-up" approach. With a MAI-like top-down agreement, basic principles are accepted and then applied uniformly to all relevant sectors. Escape from those principles requires negotiated agreements. Thus the general principle of non-discrimination gave the French (who wanted to seal off their film industry) grave difficulties, and this became an important obstacle to the successful negotiation of the treaty.

A bottom-up strategy, in contrast, does not require uniform adoption of universal policies. Non-discrimination might be a guiding principle, but the scope of the application of that princi-ple would be subject to negotiations. Only areas in which adher-ence was agreed to would be governed by the treaty. Disagreements concerning the scope of a treaty would not become deal breakers. There would simply be an agreement that the principle would not apply where there was no consensus but that it would where there was one. In this way, capital mobility could be pushed forward as far as possible with much less risk that a negotiating breakdown would leave nothing in its wake.

Obviously, a bottom-up approach is considerably less ambitious than a top-down one. But aside from the fact that the MAI was a failure and therefore an alternative strategy is needed, a bottom-up strategy does possess attractive features. The most important one is that, with it, the shared interest of all nations in the liberal treatment of capital could be accommodated without requiring an unrealistic ceding of political sovereignty. With the MAI and its top-down approach, the negotiators constantly faced a choice of either making concessions that were politically untenable at home or putting the treaty at risk. In the end, domestic politics triumphed. With the alternative bottom-up model, exemptions would not be exceptional, merely issues to work around.

The basic assumption in a bottom-up approach to international agreements is that there are shared interests that will reveal themselves and become codified without compulsion. In this case what would be assumed is that nations benefit from capital liberalization. Because of this, countries will find extensive areas where they can agree to limit or reduce barriers to capital mobility. That there are areas where consensus is absent neither vitiates the harmonization that is achieved voluntarily nor requires that compulsion be applied elsewhere. With the bottom-up approach, the contours of the agreement would reflect areas of common interest and intensity of concern. Not only would the negotiations therefore be easier, but the end of the process – the treaty itself – would reflect and respect the political preferences of the citizens of each nation. In using a bottom-up framework, trade barriers, such as those limiting FDI, would be reduced to the extent consistent with the policies, politics, and institutions of each participating country.

Bottom-up agreements would acknowledge the need for a rules-based global economic system while continuing to respect the nation as the fundamental decision-making unit in the political realm. In so doing, they would speak to at least some of the objections raised by the MAI opponents. But even a bottom-up approach to global agreements implies acceptance of the position that globalization is a process to be promoted and that its terms should be subject to multilateral agreement. Neither part of this position has been accepted by the anti-trade movement. As a result, support from that source for even bottom-up agreements to systematize the global economy is not likely in the near term.

SIX

Regulating International
Financial Markets

The MAI was flawed because it attempted to micro-manage too much. Its proponents should have been satisfied to do two things: first, articulate the general principle that each country should treat all its investors in the same way, and second, negotiate a binding agreement in the specific policy realms within which an international consensus could be achieved. Instead, the MAI advocates sought global homogeneity in governmental policies toward foreign investment. Comprehensive rules requiring universal application were to be laid down, ensuring international uniformity in the treatment of investment. All nations were to treat foreign investors in the same way.

The MAI effort to achieve international consistency failed because its negotiators could not overcome the obstacles inherent in the fact that the nation-state remains the basic unit of political decision making. The reality of differing national objectives could not be wished away. The larger lesson here is that efforts that insufficiently appreciate international diversity are doomed to frustration.

The temptation to insufficiently respect the importance of national differences is one of the problems that stands in the way of implementing a much-needed reform of the global financial system. As I will argue in this chapter, greater stability in the international financial system would enhance the benefits derived from globalization. But attempting to achieve deep financial integration, involving the creation of a global central bank and a common global currency, would be a mistake. Doing so would mean trying to achieve universal adherence to a common monetary policy. Even more than in the case of the MAI the prospects for success would be doubtful. The diversity of economic levels and of rates of inflation, unemployment, and growth present in the world today is so extensive that a single monetary policy simply cannot simultaneously be responsive to the needs of every country. This form of deep integration would therefore be economically harmful, at least to some nations. As a result, it would not be widely accepted and probably should not be.

BACKGROUND

Globalization's financial system was born on August 15, 1971, when President Richard M. Nixon ordered the United States Treasury to suspend its international purchase and sale of gold. That decision brought to an end the twenty-five-year-old Bretton Woods system of fixed exchange rates among currencies. In that system, the dollar had been positioned as the key global currency, a status that, through nearly all of the 1950s and 1960s, went unchallenged. The economies of the European countries had been devastated by the war, and dollars were greatly in demand as the continent attempted to reconstruct itself with equipment imported from the United States. Later, the dollar remained the reserve currency, in part because it alone carried a guarantee of its relationship to gold. Those who held dollars were assured that they would be able to exchange $35.00 for an ounce of gold. Because of both the continued demand for American goods and this guarantee, dollars remained the universally acceptable currency in international transactions.

The demise of Bretton Woods occurred because foreign dollar holdings became greater than could be justified by a desire to import from and invest in the United States. As a result, the guaranteed exchange for gold was increasingly exercised. The problem was that United States gold holdings were insufficient to accommodate the potential demand for the metal. Once it was exercised extensively, the right of exchange undermined the system.

Under Bretton Woods, most industrial states had controlled short-term capital movements. Because of those controls and because in normal circumstances central banks could be expected to defend established exchange rates, international currency markets were relatively inactive. Currency transactions had been confined almost exclusively to providing the means by which importers and exporters could engage in cross-border sales of goods and services. Speculative trading in currencies had been minimal. The resulting stability meant that firms could engage in international trade with little concern that either their production costs or their revenue would be affected by currency fluctuations. The cost of imported inputs would not increase or decrease due to exchange rate changes, and the same was true for the value of exports.

But after 1971, with the collapse of the old regime, "the world of international finance was changed forever" (Eatwell and Taylor 2000, 1). Now that exchange rates were allowed to change, or "float," international firms faced risks that they had not encountered before. To the extent that they either exported their products or imported intermediate goods, the firms' costs of production, and therefore their profitability, were determined at least in part by changes in exchange rates. The strengthening of a currency reduced import costs, but it also reduced exports. A weakening currency did the reverse. A new and hard-to-control element was thus introduced into the business environment.

Producers responded by trying to protect themselves, or "hedge" against, such risks. Part of normal business operations became guessing or betting about the future course of exchange rates – speculating. This was done directly in currency markets and indirectly in markets for portfolio capital.[1] In both, the fundamental strategy was the same. A firm importing inputs and anticipating that the currency of the country from which it was doing so would soon experience an increase in value would want to move quickly to buy that currency or financial instruments denominated in that currency at the current lower price. That would help the firm contain the rise in production costs that would occur when the currency of the country from which it was purchasing imports strengthened. The opposite would occur if the firm anticipated the reverse movement. If it expected a weakening, the firm would sell the currency of the country from which it was to buy inputs, awaiting the time when that currency was at a lower value and it could make purchases more cheaply. In sum, once fixed exchange rates no longer prevailed, currency markets and markets for financial instruments grew rapidly.

The international financial services sector thus entered a period of rapid growth, the pace of which accelerated during the 1980s with the adoption of the new technologies of information processing and the internet. The magnitude and rapidity of the most recent growth in global portfolio investment and currency sales are reported in Tables 6.1 and 6.2. As Table 6.1 shows, global portfolio investment as a percentage of gross domestic product almost doubled in the ten years between 1987 and 1997, growing most in the rich countries but experiencing an expansion everywhere, even among the lowest-income countries in the world. A similar increase occurred in foreign exchange markets (Table 6.2).

---

[1]   Portfolio investment refers to stocks, bonds, and bank and trade-related lending and borrowing.

TABLE 6.1. Portfolio investment[a] flows as a percentage of gross domestic product by level of development, 1987, 1997

	1987	1997
World	5.5	10.3
High-Income Countries	7.4	16.0
Upper-Middle-Income Countries	2.8	3.6
Lower-Middle-Income Countries	1.3	1.6
Low-Income Countries	1.0	1.2

[a] Portfolio Investment is equal to Gross Private Capital Flows – Gross Foreign Direct Investment.
Source: Calculated from World Bank, *World Development Indicators*, *1999*, Table 6.1.

TABLE 6.2. Average daily turnover in global foreign exchange markets (in billions of U.S. dollars), 1989–98

	1989	1992	1995	1998
Traditional Foreign Exchange Instruments	590	820	1,190	1,490
Foreign Exchange Derivative Instruments	–	–	45	97
Interest Rate Derivative Instruments	–	–	151	265
TOTAL	590	820	1,386	1,852

Source: Bank for International Settlements, "Central Bank Survey of Foreign Exchange and Derivatives Market Activity in April 1998: Preliminary Global Data," press release, Table 1. Available at ⟨http://www.bis.org/⟩. Accessed 3/19/00.

Transactions in Table 6.2 are divided into two components: traditional foreign exchange sales and derivative sales, a category for which data were collected for the first time in 1995. The very rapid growth in traditional foreign exchange sales is more than can be explained by the need to finance the import and export of goods and services. Thus much of that growth, in addition to all of the increase in the derivatives' market, occurred as a result of hedging against the uncertainties of the new currency regime.

PORTFOLIO INVESTMENT

Unlike foreign direct investment (FDI), portfolio investment – the purchase of bonds, stocks, and bank and trade-related lending – is done to seek capital appreciation as well as interest, profits, and dividends. Such investments, however, neither create new businesses nor add directly to the productive capacity of already existing firms. Nevertheless, such flows can help to expand output. When received, they have the potential to permit more investment in plant and equipment than would otherwise be the case. As Manuel R. Agosin puts its, "when a country is open to international financial flows, it no longer has to finance an increase in investment with a commensurate increase in domestic savings (and, hence, a decline in consumption)" (Agosin 1998, 1–2).

Economists generally regard the development of financial markets in a favorable light, though they are increasingly sensitive to the associated risks. Barry Eichengreen is representative. He believes that "liberalized financial markets have compelling benefits ... [since] they encourage savings mobilization and efficient investment allocation." Eichengreen writes that "compared to the earlier era, when developing countries repressed private financial transactions and governments employed policies of directed credit to dictate resource allocation, there are clear efficiency gains from relying on the market." Nevertheless, he goes on, "notwithstanding the manifest benefits of financial liberalization, capital markets are characterized by information asymmetries that can give rise to overshooting, sharp corrections, and, in the extreme, financial crises." The resulting instability, Eichengreen concludes, "provides a compelling argument for erecting a financial safety net" either at the international level or by individual countries (Eichengreen 1999, 2, 3).

There is no questioning the empirical fact that greater financial instability exists in the recently created environment of capital market liberalization than existed previously. Eatwell and Taylor provide a list of recent financial disruptions that includes a crisis in Latin America between 1979 and 1981, the developing country debt crisis initiated in 1982, a financial crisis in Mexico in 1994–95, the Asian crisis of 1997–98, a dramatic default on outstanding loans by Russia in 1998, and a massive currency devaluation in Brazil in 1999 (Eatwell and Taylor 2000, 5). In a working paper that he prepared for the Bank for International Settlements (BIS), William R. White writes, "both the frequency and severity of international financial crises seems to have been rising over the last twenty years or so." Moreover, he continues, "financial crises have increasingly led to severe economic disruption, increases in unemployment and even a return to poverty for many in some emerging markets" (White 2000, 1).

In fact, the damage done by these financial crises has been immense. Most recently, as the World Bank has reported, "the negative social impact of the East Asian crisis and consequent crises in Russia and Brazil has been enormous" (World Bank 2000, 47). Table 6.3 illustrates this impact. In 1998, the year after the onset of the Asian crisis, output plummeted and poverty soared. Indonesia's economy, for example, was decimated, with production falling by 15.1 percent in 1998 compared to 1997, and the experience of Thailand was nearly as devastating. The result was a reversal of the long-term trend in these countries of declining poverty rates.

TABLE 6.3. Growth rate of real gross domestic product (GDP) per capita and poverty rate for selected East Asian countries, 1997, 1998

	GDP Growth Rate[a]				National Poverty Rate[b]	
	1965–97	1997	1998	1987	1997	1998
Indonesia	4.8	2.9	–15.1	17.4	11.0	16.7
Malaysia	4.1	5.4	–9.2	15.5[c]	8.2	NA
Rep. of Korea	6.7	4.5	–6.7	NA	8.6	19.2
Thailand	5.1	–1.4	–10.3	18.0[d]	9.8	12.9

[a] 1965–97: GNP per capita.
[b] 1997–98: Indonesia: National Poverty Line equivalent to about $1 a day in 1985 (International Purchasing Parity); Malaysia: income poverty; Republic of Korea: National Poverty Line equivalent to about $4 per day in 1985 IPP dollars; Thailand: National Income poverty measured at around $2 a day.
[c] 1989.
[d] 1990.

Source: 1965–97 GNP per capita: World Bank, *World Development Indicators, 1999*, Table 1.4; 1997–98 GDP Per Capita Growth Rate: World Bank, *Global Economic Prospects and the Developing Countries, 2000*, Table 2.1.

Even the International Monetary Fund (IMF) concedes, in the words of Manuel Guitian, the director of its Monetary and Exchange Affairs Department, that unconstrained capital flows "expose countries to external disturbances and can have a destabilizing effect." Guitian continues, "the dangers of sudden *outflows* are well understood, but capital *inflows* also carry risks – they may create difficulties for monetary policy management and inflation control as well as for exchange rate stability and export competitiveness" (emphasis in original; Guitian 1998, 14). Similarly, in a 1997 paper, the IMF's research department staff reported that there were two reasons for tempering optimism about port-folio financing. First, the global market for investments like these might change. A change in the business cycle in the developed world or a "financial disturbance, such as a sudden drop in equity prices," could provoke a large-scale sell-off of stocks. Under such circumstances the flow of portfolio investment to the developing world might suddenly dry up. The consequences of such a drop-off in investment could be calamitous, leaving a country suddenly without the financial resources necessary to sustain its current levels of consumption and production. The second reason is that a country with a fixed exchange rate might experience a specula-tive attack on its currency. If that were to occur, it might create so much uncertainty that the capital inflow would essentially be shut off (International Monetary Fund Research Department Staff 1997, 12).

In fact in the run-up to Asia's financial crisis, short-term capital had become increasingly important in the region's financial markets. The setting was one in which high domestic interest rates were combined with fixed exchange rates in an inadequately reg-ulated financial system. This combination encouraged short-term borrowing from abroad, particularly since a stable exchange rate implied that there was no need to be concerned about the possi-bility that a depreciating currency would increase the real burden of debt.

In these circumstances, the growth of private sector debt meant that when a random downturn in confidence occurred, short-term capital fled the region, resulting in the already high interest rates' rising even more. Defaults and bankruptcies ensued, reinforcing the tendency for investors to flee. This rush, in turn, put pressure on the presumably fixed exchange rates, which, when they could no longer be defended, resulted in an even greater flight of capital as investors attempted to avoid the loss of wealth associated with a depreciating currency. To restrain the outward tide of capital, central bankers followed the advice of the IMF and raised interest rates, hoping thereby to offset the panic experienced by investors. The problem was that to overcome investor panic required that interest levels be so high that they all but precluded credit market activity. Loans became too expensive to be attractive, and interest rates too high to allow repayment. In the end, therefore, a major economic collapse triggered by developments in the financial markets was experienced.

The Asian economies might have been able to avoid such damage if they had moved to limit capital's ability to flee, while judiciously raising interest rates and allowing exchange rates to fall moderately. Such a combination might have preempted the panic and induced capital to remain in the region. Failing this, there was really no way monetary authorities could have prevented investors from moving their capital from the region, in the process putting the exchange rate under severe downward pressure. There is, of course, no certainty that limiting capital mobility would have worked. But the point remains that if the movement of funds had been more subject to discipline, the upward movement in interest rates and the downward movement in exchange rates could have been more moderate than the radical movements that actually occurred, the results of what one economist, based in Thailand, described as "the frenzied and increasingly irrational movements of capital" (*Economist* 1998, 2). Less hyperactivity among investors, compelled by controls, might have allowed the underlying strength of the Asian economies to figure more prominently in investment decisions. If so, the damage might have been minimized.

OPEN CAPITAL MARKETS

Why would a country choose to risk instability and punishing financial panics by opening its capital markets? The answer is the

TABLE 6.4. Changes in per capita financial flows,[a] foreign direct investment (FDI) and gross domestic product (GDP), 1990–97

	Change in per Capita Financial Flows	Change in per Capita FDI	Percentage Change GDP
Latin America and the Caribbean	84.10	61.37	3.3
Europe and Central Asia	19.52	28.97	−5.4
East Asia and the Pacific	15.40	27.88	9.9
Middle East and North Africa	9.16	−7.77	2.6
Sub-Saharan Africa	5.94	4.09	2.1
South Asia	3.67	−0.07	5.7

[a] Summation of bonds, equity investments, and bank and trade-related lending.
Source: Change in Per Capita Financial Flows and FDI calculated from World Bank, *World Development Indicators 1998*, Tables 6.8 and 1.1; Percentage Change GDP calculated from *World Development Report 1998/99*, Table 11.

exaggerated belief of policy makers in the benefits that accrue from doing so. Table 6.4 points to the issues involved. On the one hand, the data suggest that when a country opens itself to receive financial capital inflows, FDI arrives as well. That is, there seems to be a positive relationship between open financial markets and FDI inflows. The Latin American and Caribbean region was the recipient of more financial capital and more FDI than any other region. The next largest recipients of financial capital, Europe and Central Asia and East Asia and the Pacific, also were the beneficiaries of considerably more FDI than the Middle East, North Africa, sub-Saharan Africa, and South Asia. What these data suggest is that maintaining liberal capital markets pays off with relatively high inflows of both FDI as well as short-term capital.

On the other hand, openness to overseas capital is not unambiguously associated with economic growth. Thus East Asia and the Pacific received far less capital from overseas than did Latin America and the Caribbean but grew at three times the rate. South Asia received very little foreign capital but nonetheless experienced rapid growth, in excess of five percent per year. Finally, the countries in transition from socialism in Europe and Central Asia received a considerable influx of both financial capital and FDI but nevertheless at the same time experienced economic decline.

In short, at least with respect to economic growth, Jagdish Bhagwati almost certainly is right when he says "the claims of enormous benefits from free capital mobility are not persuasive" (Bhagwati 1998, 7). Capital account liberalization enhances the likelihood that a country will receive short-term capital inflows. These inflows are useful in supporting levels of consumption and investment that might otherwise be unattainable. Doing so also increases the probability that foreign direct investment will be received and with it enhanced access to advanced technology, management, and overseas markets. But at the same time, that very process of liberalization exposes a country to the threat of "hot money" speculative attacks on its currency – attacks that, as we have seen in East Asia, can devastate an economy. And all of this occurs without a systematic positive effect on economic growth.

But for many poor countries the choice of current account liberalization was no choice at all. It was imposed on them by the IMF or the World Bank or both as a condition for financial assistance. Opening markets to short-term capital was almost always a component of the structural adjustment programs (SAPs) the IMF insisted upon when a country asked for assistance. These

SAPs were first imposed during the late 1970s and early 1980s when a combination of falling commodity prices and high and rising interest rates drove numerous countries to the precipice of default on external loans.

To be sure, even critics such as Lance Taylor and Ute Pieper believed that the SAPs contained "a fair proportion of the useful policy suggestions that the economics profession has to offer." But as Taylor and Pieper pointed out, the policies also contained a very important blind spot. SAPs were oblivious to the risks associated with current account liberalization. As these analysts put it, there was "little discussion in the 1980s about the need for prudential regulation of money and capital markets – for careful audits by the authorities of the risk and performance of portfolios combined with sanctions on financial institutions in trouble" (Taylor and Pieper 1996, 7, 12). As Alan Greenspan acknowledged, "more investment monies flowed into these economies than could be profitably employed at reasonable risk" (quoted in *Economist* 1998, 1).

REFORM

The conventional wisdom that market liberalization is all that is required to promote prosperity is obviously in need of revision (Rodrik 1999, 23–66). Indeed, what has emerged, especially in the immediate aftermath of the 1997–98 Asian financial crisis, was a period in which, as Kenneth Rogoff wrote, it was "hard to open a business newspaper or magazine . . . without confronting another sweeping proposal to reform the 'international financial architecture.'" The list of proposed reforms compiled by Rogoff includes the formation of an international deposit insurance corporation, an international bankruptcy court, controls over capital inflows or outflows or both, a global regulator of financial markets and institutions, and a world central bank. As Rogoff concedes, "many of these ideas are not new, but they are being vented more forcefully, and taken more seriously, than at any time since Harry Dexter White and John Maynard Keynes masterminded the creation of the World Bank and the International Monetary Fund at the Bretton Woods conference at the end of World War II" (Rogoff 1999, 1).

The theoretical case for financial market regulation rests on the obvious fact that participants in financial markets do not take into account the potential social costs of their actions. Those unaccounted costs are what economists call negative externalities. As Eatwell and Taylor put it, "taking risks is what financial institutions are for. But markets reflect the private calculations of risk, and so tend to under-price the risk faced by society as a whole" (Eatwell and Taylor 2000, 17–18). Because they do not bear these costs, investors take more risks than they would if they were burdened by the full weight of the consequences of their actions. The purpose of regulating financial markets is to ensure that behavior that imposes excessive risks on society is curbed. This would be done by having traders internalize what are now external costs – that is, have more of the social costs associated with speculative behavior borne by those in the market. The fundamental problem is that while this process of increasing internalized costs and therefore reducing social risk is frequently undertaken by national regulatory agencies, no counterpart to their efforts exists at the international level. According to Eatwell and Taylor, while "today, financial markets know no borders . . . regulatory power remains trapped within increasingly irrelevant national boundaries" (Eatwell and Taylor 2000, 6).

There is a strong temptation to consider the implementation of international financial regulations as simply the logical extension of the regulatory process that has occurred at the national level. It is in this way that Eatwell and Taylor come to advocate a world financial authority (WFA) and that Jeffrey E. Garten argues for a global central bank. For Garten, "today's chaotic international market mirrors how the American economy evolved between the Civil War and the 1930s." Citing "booms and busts, countless bank failures, [and] rampant bankruptcies," he maintains that in response "over time the United States set up crucial central institutions – the Securities and Exchange Commission in 1933, the Federal Deposit Insurance Corp[oration]in 1934, and most important, the Federal Reserve in 1913." What emerged was "a managed national economy," and "this is what now must occur on a global scale" (Garten 1998, 1).

The invocation of the experience of individual nations, however, is not really helpful in pointing the way to effective mechanisms of control at the international level. The reason this is so is found precisely in the nature of the globalization process itself. As we have seen in the MAI context, the advance of integrated global markets does not create by itself the conditions that allow deep integration. While advancing technology and the logic of global market integration seem to cry out for supra-national regulatory authority, the locus of political decision making and the basic unit of self-government in the contemporary world remain national. Even with globalization, the nation-state is the basic unit of accountability. While markets may be global, politics and administration are not. Because this is so, transnational institution building has advanced far more slowly than the pace that the technology of globalization alone would seem to call for.

The tension between the globalizing tendencies of the new technology and the continuing salience of national sovereignty can be seen in Garten's proposals. Garten explicitly supports establishing a global central bank, but he makes no mention of a universal monetary union. This omission is all but fatal to his proposal, since the use of a common currency within the jurisdiction of a central bank's authority is critical to its effectiveness.[2] Further, Garten's attempted reassurance to his American readership that a global central bank would not operate within the United States and "would not be able to override the decisions of our central bank" reveals the limited scope and authority of the institution he defends. This limitation on the international bank's ability to override more parochial institutions would presumably exist for other entities as well, such as, for example, the European Union (Garten 1998, 2). In effect, Garten concedes the limitations of the national analogy that drives his own suggestion.

Eatwell and Taylor are forced to do the same for their proposed WFA. They do not conceive of the WFA as either a world central bank or even a lender of last resort; its role would be to regulate capital markets. To be effective, Eatwell and Taylor write, a WFA would "need to perform the same tasks performed today by efficient national regulators, namely information, authorization, surveillance, guidance, enforcement and policy" (Eatwell and Taylor 2000, 220). Yet at least as proposed by Eatwell and Taylor, the effectiveness of a WFA would be constrained by the intentions and competencies of national authorities. Most of the functions Eatwell and Taylor enumerate for the WFA "would in reality be performed by national authorities acting in conjunction with and as agents for the WFA." They continue, "the importance of the WFA is in its harmonizing of standards and procedures and developing the global scope and relevance of decision-making" (221). The WFA would not establish its own enforcement department, "rather it [would] . . . take the lead in coordinating the enforcement activities of national regulators involved in international cases" (223).

The problem with this is that it is precisely among those countries where domestic regulatory mechanisms are weakest that the role of the WFA would be most important. But since the WFA's

[2] This is why the European Central Bank has created the Euro.

regulatory strength would be dependent upon the competence of local authorities, there would be great risk that the institutional foundation supporting the WFA would be too insubstantial to allow it to carry out its assigned tasks effectively. Eatwell and Taylor recognize the difficulty. They write that

> nowhere will the WFA confront greater problems than in dealing with the financial regulatory problems of developing and transition economies. Their own regulatory capacities are underdeveloped, they lack a suitable number of qualified personnel, and, given their small size relative to the volume of international financial transactions, the risks they confront are proportionately far greater than those of the US, Europe, or Japan. (227)

The response by Eatwell and Taylor to these problems is at best only hopeful. They would have the developed nations provide technical assistance to train regulators in poor countries. In addition, they anticipate that poor countries would move to upgrade their standards and capacities, prodded by the fact that the availability of low-interest loans from rich countries would be contingent upon stringent regulatory systems being in place (228).

But even if it were possible to be optimistic and to believe that the regulatory regime in poor countries could be upgraded rapidly, the problem of the instability associated with unregulated capital flows would remain. Joseph Stiglitz, a senior vice president and chief economist at the World Bank during the mid-1990s, points to the need for the creation of "financial systems that buffer the economy against shocks rather than magnifying the shocks" (Stiglitz 1998, 12). To do this it would be desirable to increase the inflow of FDI compared to short-term capital and to reduce the volatility of short-term capital movements. If accomplished, each would augment a country's capital stock, while reducing its vulnerability to rapid capital flights.

To achieve this objective, however, it is necessary to reduce the profitability of short-term investments relative to long-term commitments and FDI. Two different approaches have been offered to accomplish this end. The first is widely referred to as the Tobin Tax, since it was first suggested by the economist James Tobin in 1978. Such a tax would take the form of, as Tobin originally put it, "an internationally agreed uniform tax, say 1%, on all spot conversions of one currency into another" (Tobin quoted in Kaul, Grunberg, and ul Haq 1996, 1). The theory behind the tax is that by raising the cost of moving funds from one country to another such flows would be reduced.

The second strategy would be for individual countries to adopt a policy similar to the one employed by Chile between 1991 and 1997, when that nation imposed a one-year reserve requirement on capital inflows. Referred to as an unremunerated reserve requirement (URR), the Chilean policy mandated a one-year compulsory 20 percent deposit for capital inflows. These "reserves" did not earn interest during the year that they were on deposit at the country's central bank (Nadal-De Simone and Sorsa 1999, 11). The anticipation is that reducing the earnings on investments of one year or less in this way would discourage such short-term flows.

The Tobin Tax, unlike the URR, has never been implemented. Nevertheless, its probable efficacy is not much in dispute. As pointed out in an overview of an academic symposium on the Tobin Tax, "the authors agree that the tax would certainly deter trades with a short-term horizon because it would make the movement of large sums of money quickly in and out of a country more costly" (Kaul et al., 5). As noted, the URR has been implemented, and Stiglitz reports that "even most critics of the Chilean system acknowledge that it has significantly lengthened the maturity composition of capital inflows to Chile" (Stiglitz 1998, 15; but see Nadal-De Simone and Sorsa 1999, 48, for evidence of avoidance of the URR).

RESISTANCE TO CHANGE

Support for market intervention of the kind suggested by the Tobin Tax and the URR reached a high tide in the aftermath of the Asian financial crisis of 1997–98. Bhagwati, an ardent defender of liberal trade in goods and services, led the charge. In a much quoted article in *Foreign Affairs*, he declared that "only an untutored economist will argue that . . . free trade in widgets and life insurance policies is the same as free capital mobility." He went on to denounce "the Washington-Treasury complex," those economists and public officials who exaggerate the beneficial effects of free capital mobility "while simultaneously failing to evaluate its crisis-prone downside" (Bhagwati 1998, 10). According to Bhagwati, the opposition to limiting short-term capital mobility results in part from exaggerated claims on behalf of free market theory. It was not, however, only a problem of misplaced economic theory:

> interests have also played a central role. Wall Street's financial firms have obvious self-interest in a world of free capital mobility since it only enlarges the arena in which to make money. It is not surprising therefore that Wall Street has put its powerful oar into the turbulent water of Washington political lobbying to steer in this direction. (Bhagwati 1998, 11)

Almost certainly, in their advocacy of unrestricted capital markets Wall Street lobbyists are pushing on an open door. The very individuals they are lobbying – the people in economic decision-making positions, particularly those in the United States government – are themselves frequently past and likely future participants in the financial sector of the economy. Bhagwati concludes that "this powerful network . . . is unable to look much beyond the interest of Wall Street which it equates with the good of the world" (Bhagwati 1998, 12).

For a brief moment after the Asian crisis, the Russian default, and the devaluation of the Brazilian real, it nevertheless did appear that the world was ready to move toward the regulation of short-term capital. The 1999 *Economic Report of the President* called for the "reform of the International Financial Architecture," noting that the United States had proposed reforms "designed to reduce the incidence of future crises" and with the aim of creating "an international financial system for the 21st century that captures the full benefits of global markets and capital flows, while minimizing the risk of disruptions and better protecting the most vulnerable groups in society" (*Economic Report of the President, 1999*, Chapter 7, 1).

This official enthusiasm for reform waned quickly, however. One year after the 1999 report had declared the need to change the international financial system, the 2000 edition of *The Economic Report of the President* all but reversed course. It continued to emphasize the need for national regulatory regimes but underplayed the need for change at the international level. It declared that "a central lesson of the crises of the 1990's is that countries largely shape their own destinies. Hence, building a sound global financial system requires that individual countries work to ensure that their financial systems and macroeconomic policies are sound, consistent, and transparent" (*Economic Report of the President, 2000*, 228; see Box 6–3 for recommendations, 229).

William R. White reported on the retreat from global reform in his paper for the BIS. According to White, despite the fact that global financial integration has resulted in "a heightened tendency to financial instability and even sporadic crisis . . . it is notable that most of the thinking surrounding the search for a 'New International Financial Architecture' has resulted (less grandly) in suggestions for only incremental changes to the current system" (White 2000, 27).

For the time being, perhaps until the next crisis again under-scores the fragility of the financial foundations of globalization, it is likely that nothing much will be done to strengthen international financial architecture. Complacency, combined with free market ideology and the power of the "Washington Treasury Complex," has beaten back efforts to reform this weakness in globalization. The destructive potential of "hot money" persists, threatening to undo the economic gains achieved in relatively poor nations as the new technology for communications and transportation facilitates the spread of economic development.

Unfortunately, the shattering impact of unstable financial markets almost certainly will be experienced again sometime in the near future. The place and circumstances of the event are, of course, uncertain. But there is little doubt that the failure to move ahead with market intervention means that serious vulnerabilities will persist in the global financial system. The onset of the next crisis is really only a question of when and where, not whether.

Stabilizing the global financial system is a political issue. Those in favor of it will have to mobilize powerful popular support to overcome the entrenched and self-interested efforts of financial communities and their supportive governments. Furthermore, the reforms will have to be carefully shaped. They will have to be suf-ficiently robust to alter behavior enough so as to reduce the like-lihood of financial panics. At the same time, they will have to be sensitive to the requirement that they not impede the resource-mobilizing tasks that financial markets are capable of achieving.

Recognition of the threat posed by speculators need not be viewed as a reason to turn away from the potential represented by global economic integration. But for that integration to yield its growth-associated benefits, financial panics must be minimized if not eliminated. What is needed is financial market reform that avoids the straitjacket of supra-national central banks or regula-tory agencies and, at the same time, rejects the untenable view that

95

injurious financial instability is inevitable. The Tobin Tax and URR point to means by which the volatility associated with financial market integration can be brought under control, even as financial markets are allowed to continue to facilitate global economic growth.

SEVEN

The Student Anti-Sweatshop Movement

The technology that has permitted globalization has not only facilitated the movement of goods and services, FDI, and financial
instruments. It has also made it easier for people to move across
borders. The increased speed and reduced cost of transportation
have been particularly important in this. So too has been the spread
of economic growth. That process not only raises income levels,
thereby facilitating travel, but also causes the dislocations that
often compel the need to relocate. Beyond all of this, advances in
communications have also encouraged migration. As people learn
about and aspire to the higher standards of living experienced
elsewhere, they are more likely to migrate.

It is no surprise, consequently, to learn that immigration rates
to the United States have steadily increased in the years since
World War II. During the 1990s that rate was 3.6 per 1,000 of the
United States population. By comparison the rate was 1.7 during
the 1960s, 2.1 in the 1970s, and 3.1 during the 1980s (U.S.
Census Bureau 2000, Table 5, p. 19). Furthermore, the United
States is not alone in experiencing increased population inflows.
The foreign population as a percentage of the total population
increased in sixteen of seventeen European countries for which

the World Bank provides data on the subject (World Bank 2001, Table 6.13).

What is of interest is that this increased migration has occurred in the absence of any global agreement to promote the flow of people among nations. Nothing like a GATT or a WTO exists to promote and regularize the movement of people. To fill this void, Jagdish Bhagwati has suggested the creation of a World Migration Organization (WMO). But this proposal has not gained official endorsement, and in any case, the organization he proposes would have very limited powers. Restricted to periodic country reviews, the construction of burden-sharing indices, and the development of codes for the rights and obligations of different types of immigrants, its mandate would be insignificant compared to the WTO's responsibilities concerning the movement of goods and services (Bhagwati 1998, 315–17). Migration, in short, has largely remained untouched by the rules that govern other aspects of globalization. Saskia Sassen is right that in today's globalization there is a tension between "the growing pressures toward multilateralism and internationalism, on the one hand, and the ongoing insistence on unilateral action when it comes to immigration issues, on the other" (Sassen 2000, 69).

The explanation for this neglect does not lie in a disapproval of migration in economic theory. To the contrary, economic principles support the free flow of labor across borders. Economic theory teaches that labor is an input in production in the same way that capital is. Therefore it follows that free markets are the appropriate institutions through which to allocate labor resources. Allowing workers to respond to differences in wages is the way to ensure that both scarcities and oversupplies are reduced and that workers find jobs suited to their skills. Just as economic theory argues for the breaking down of barriers to the mobility of capital in the name of efficient deployment, it makes the same case for labor. A multilateral organization to champion and regulate such a process seems to be called for.

The reason that there is no WMO is that a strong political coalition calling for its creation has not formed. To begin with, a grouping of powerful corporate managers of the kind that worked on behalf of establishing the WTO does not exist for immigration. Labor scarcity simply has not been a sufficiently important problem for elites to mount a campaign to create a WMO. At the same time, a formidable opposition to unrestricted immigration does exist. This group is concerned that such a labor inflow would become a torrent that would put unacceptable downward pressure on wage rates. As we have seen, the mere existence of overseas workers ready and able to work in industries that could compete with those in the United States makes it more difficult for the domestic labor force to raise its wages. Clearly, a greatly increased presence of immigrants within this country would only intensify that difficulty. Finally, and perhaps most decisively, the interests of the potential migrants are not considered in the national politics that would see a proposed WMO as part of a liberal migration regime. Obviously, would-be immigrants would favor such a policy orientation. But their voices are not given expression or weight in the receiving country's political discourse on the subject.

Without a WMO, it is likely that migration rates are lower than they would be if such an organization existed. An important consequence of this attenuated flow of people is that it impairs the ability of the global poor to raise their income levels. The disparities in wage levels between the countries of origin and the countries that would receive a population inflow are very large. An enhanced ability to migrate would therefore increase the opportunity for workers residing in poor countries to raise their standard of living. This would be true even if downward pressure on the wage levels in the developed countries resulted from the increased supply of migrant workers. In short, because global migration is not free, labor mobility is effective only to a limited extent in overcoming third world poverty.

Since a liberal global migration system is politically untenable, advocates on behalf of the interests of the third world poor have had to look elsewhere to devise approaches to raise living standards. In many ways the most interesting of these efforts has been the student anti-sweatshop movement. This movement is a good-faith attempt to address the inequalities present in the emerging global labor system. It draws its energy from the belief that American universities are accomplices in an exploitative global labor system. What the movement seeks to do is redress the poor working conditions and low wages experienced by workers employed in the apparel industry in poor countries. In its efforts, this movement has generally avoided the pitfalls of the unilateralism and localism characteristic of the anti-globalization movement.

Notwithstanding its good intentions, however, the anti-sweatshop movement has failed to devise a strategy to achieve its goal of alleviating poverty. This failure is rooted in the students' failure to grapple seriously with the economics of underdevelopment or to consider the ways in which globalization could be shaped to advance the interests of the world's poor. Instead, the movement advocates interventions by non-governmental organizations, a strategy that is unlikely to have a significant impact on the problem. Neglected are the two policy interventions – the opening of markets for the products of the third world and a global governance system that promotes labor rights – that would go farthest in achieving the goal the movement seeks, that of labor empowerment.

POLICING THE INDUSTRY

The student anti-sweatshop movement is rooted in a series of disclosures, in 1995 and 1996, that brought to light shocking labor conditions in the apparel industry. Sweatshops were found in Central America producing clothing for The Gap and Kathie Lee Gifford's Wal-Mart line and in Indonesia producing Nike shoes. Further unfavorable public notice resulted from a raid by the United States Department of Labor on a compound in El Monte in Southern California in which seventy-two undocumented immigrants were discovered working in a condition of peonage (Ross 1997, 26–29). In response, in August 1996, on the initiative of the Clinton administration, the Apparel Industry Partnership (AIP) was created to address the issue of sweatshops. Its membership included prominent apparel firms, non-profit organizations working in the field, and two unions – the Union of Needletrades, Industrial and Textile Employees (UNITE) and the Retail, Wholesale and Department Store Union. AIP issued an interim report in April 1997 and a final agreement in November 1998. In that agreement, members of the AIP agreed to create a non-profit organization, the Fair Labor Association (FLA), "to oversee monitoring of compliance" with the Workplace Code of Conduct that had been agreed to in April 1997 (Apparel Industry Partnership 1999, 1).

A draft of the Collegiate Code of Conduct for firms producing licensed merchandise was issued as part of this agreement. In the draft, standards concerning working hours, overtime compensation, and health and safety conditions were proposed for the licensed apparel industry. The code prohibited the use of child labor, forced labor, discrimination, and harassment and abuse. The draft agreement also included the provision that "licensees shall recognize and respect the right of employees to freedom of association and collective bargaining" (Collegiate Code of Conduct 1998, 2).

The proposals in the draft drew the opposition of the union members of the AIP. Instead of the "living wage" that the unions wanted, the clause in the draft called upon licensees to pay "as a floor, at least the minimum wage required by local law or the local prevailing industry wage, whichever is higher, and shall provide legally mandated benefits" (Collegiate Code of Conduct 1998, III. B. 1). The provisions of the draft emphasized self-monitoring and self-enforcement to ensure compliance with the agreement, in contrast to an independent external overview sought by the dissenters. Furthermore, according to the draft, company names and locations were to be made available to the Collegiate Licensing Company, but only on a confidential basis (Collegiate Code of Conduct 1998, IV. A. 4). Though the draft declared that its adherents were committed to "conducting periodic announced and unannounced visits . . . to survey compliance with the Code," the results of these visits were to be kept private. Finally, instead of all plants being subject to investigation, only a sampling of production facilities were to be visited, and they by as yet unnamed inspectors (Collegiate Code of Conduct 1998, V. A). As a result of their objections to these provisions, UNITE, the retail workers' union, and the Interfaith Center on Corporate Responsibility all quit the group.

Mark Levinson of UNITE defended his union's withdrawal from the FLA by saying "This agreement is not very good. How can you talk about eliminating sweatshops without making a commitment to pay a living wage?" Alan Howard, also speaking for UNITE, declared that "the monitoring is badly flawed. We don't think it's very independent monitoring and the companies pick their monitors and the factories to be monitored so there won't be surprise inspections" (Greenhouse 1998, 2). Michael Shellenberger, a spokesman for Global Exchange, summarized the objections to the agreement: "This is a step backwards. These companies will be able to market their products as sweatshop-free – without actually making changes to sweatshop practices abroad" (Dobnik 1998, 5).[1]

---

[1] Criticism has come from the other side as well. Some corporate producers reject the agreement as too demanding. According to a report in the *New*

Notwithstanding these objections, the Collegiate Code of Conduct draft won the immediate endorsement of 17 universities, including Duke and Notre Dame, pioneers in university codes of conduct (Greenhouse 1999). Seventeen soon swelled to more than 100, and by the end of 2000, 148 (Fair Labor Association 2000). A number of other schools, however, refrained from signing on, arguing that the draft provisions were inadequate. Included in this group were the University of Michigan, the University of Wisconsin, and the University of California (Appelbaum and Dreier 1999, 77).

The student activists as represented by Students Against Sweatshops also rejected the FLA. As an alternative they established the Worker Rights Consortium (WRC), which, by November 20, 2000, claimed sixty-six college and university adherents (Worker Rights Consortium 2000, 1). The difference between the FLA and the WRC lies less in the content of their respective codes of conduct than in the goals of each organization. The FLA wants to resolve the sweatshop issue by securing consensus and the cooperation of all parties, including the industry. In contrast, the WRC, as it declares in its draft document, represents:

> a conceptual and practical alternative to industry-controlled monitoring organizations. United Students Against Sweatshops is convinced that, no matter how well intentioned these organizations may be, their effect will be to relieve the pressure to clean up the industry, to cover up abuses and to lend the credibility of a University's name to the very companies that have created the global sweatshop system. (Worker Rights Consortium 2000a, 7)

York Times, the FLA "has encountered problems attracting corporate members." Objectors cited the risk that they would be embarrassed if monitors uncover violations, their reluctance to absorb the costs involved with compliance, and their reluctance to be assessed for the costs of monitoring (Greenhouse 1999, 1–2).

Fundamentally separating the two organizations is the students' rejection of collaboration with manufacturers in certifying the presence of acceptable working conditions.

Instead, the WRC proposes a system in which member schools would require affidavits from their licensees that their contractors and sub-contractors are in compliance with a code of conduct. The content of the code is not specified by the WRC, though the organization stipulates that it "must include provisions such as a living wage, the right to organize and collective bargaining, protecting workers' health and safety, compliance with local laws, protection of women's rights, and prohibitions on child labor, forced labor and forced overtime" (Worker Rights Consortium 2000a, 4).

To verify compliance, the WRC would undertake spot checks on working conditions. These investigations would be funded by the member universities from the money earned through licensing. Though the WRC would have responsibility for the investigations, it "does not aim to set up a permanent system of factory policing." Rather its intention is to "work in partnership with indigenous worker-allied groups when carrying out investigations and research initiatives." In this, it hopes "to build capacity and open up the space for workers and their allies to advocate on their own behalf" (Worker Rights Consortium 2000a, 6).

It would be left to the universities themselves to determine the penalties to be applied when a licensee is either not in compliance or has failed to disclose required information. The WRC, however, would "establish a system of guidelines for such penalties with which to advise participating universities that wish to impose sanctions in response to violation." In this, though termination of a licensing agreement "is not a first step in response to violations," the WRC insists that "[it] must be one that universities are willing to take" (Worker Rights Consortium 2000a, 6).

Two members of the WRC advisory board have elaborated on the organization's intentions. According to Richard P. Appelbaum and Edna Bonacich, the WRC sees the sweatshop issue as one of worker empowerment, and it has shaped both its organizational structure and policies to achieve that end. They write that "only with power can workers resist the inevitable tendency of global competition to drive down wages." In its effort "to give workers power, the WRC will contact non-governmental organizations, religious groups and unions in the areas where there are factories." These "local advocates will inform workers of their rights under local laws, as well as about any codes of conduct to which manufacturers have agreed, so that the workers can speak up when their rights are violated." Unannounced factory visits will be carried out by such sympathetic NGOs. But "in the long run, the consortium's approach means helping to create a safe environment, where workers can organize independent unions and engage in collective bargaining, if they choose" (Appelbaum and Bonacich 2000, B5).

The WRC made no provision for corporate membership on its governing board and offered no role for firms in the selection of monitors. Indeed, the organization adopted an adversarial stance toward brand-name manufacturers. It is not clear, however, that the university adherents to the WRC fully understood the shift in strategy that the new organization represented compared to the FLA. When Philip H. Knight, the chairman of Nike, reacted to the University of Oregon's announcement of adherence to the WRC by declaring that he would no longer contribute to his alma mater, school officials seemed genuinely surprised at the vehemence of his reaction. Their comments suggest that Knight may have been better informed concerning the WRC strategy than was the university. Duncan McDonald, the university's vice president for public affairs and development, was reported as having said that "the university and Nike share a common goal of having a single code of conduct and a single monitoring system." Almost certainly this was an expression of wishful thinking. To talk of common goals more nearly corresponds to the approach taken by the FLA than it does to the more confrontational one taken by the WRC (Van Der Werf 2000, A43). As Liza Featherstone has put it, in defending the new strategy, "If the WRC develops as the students hope, it will help give workers and unions a stronger voice in the apparel industry, rather than simply conferring a *Good Housekeeping*-style seal of approval on 'sweat-free' brands" (Featherstone 2000, 18).

THE GLOBALIZATION OF APPAREL

To assess the usefulness of the student approach, it is necessary to examine the changing structure of the worldwide clothing industry. University-licensed apparel is the segment of the industry that in recent years has become most globalized. This segment produces standardized merchandise, apparel that does not frequently change in design or appearance. Because producers in this sector do not concern themselves with rapidly changing consumer tastes, they can undertake production far from their market outlets without worrying that the time lag between production and sale will result in the accumulation of undesired inventory (Singer 1997, 125–26).

The magnitude of globalization in this industry is illustrated by the data in Table 7.1. It is true that total employment in the industry worldwide was stable over these years, at close to 4.9 million employees. But this stability masks the fact that these were years of dramatic change in the geographic pattern of employment. Over 850,000 jobs were lost in the developed world. That number was matched by growth in the third world, more than four-fifths of which occurred in Asia. The Asian countries in which clothing employment growth was most dramatic – totaling 500,000 jobs – were Bangladesh, Thailand, Indonesia, and the Philippines. Among the developed countries, the United States lost the largest number of clothing jobs, though the percentage decrease in such employ-

TABLE 7.1. Employment in clothing industry, by region, 1980, 1992[a]

Region	1980	1992	Change
Asia	617,210	1,306,864	689,654
Latin America	550,017	502,573	−47,444
Middle East and Africa	219,337	431,076	211,739
TOTAL THIRD WORLD	1,386,564	2,240,513	853,949
Developed Countries	3,482,198	2,629,375	−852,823
TOTAL	4,868,762	4,869,888	1,126

[a] The data used in this table are for International Standard Industrial Classification Sector 322, "clothing," defined as "all wearing apparel, except footwear, manufactured by cutting and sewing fabrics, leather, fur and other materials, as well as hat bodies, hats and other millinery, fur apparel, accessories and trimmings etc." The table provides information for fifty-five countries, excluding the countries of the former Soviet bloc: Bulgaria, Czech Republic, Czechoslovakia, East Germany, Hungary, Poland, Romania, and the USSR. The year 1992 is the last one for which relatively complete data are available, as of August 2001.

Source: International Labour Organization, Globalization of the Footwear, Textiles and Clothing Industries (Geneva: ILO, 1996), Table 3.3, pp. 36–37.

ment was higher in the other countries that saw big decreases in clothing employment: France, Germany, and the United Kingdom, as well as the nations of Latin America. It was Brazil that accounted for nearly all of Latin America's decline.

Though data on wage rates are scarce, it is clear that the pattern of industrial relocation reflected a search by producers for inexpensive labor. The industrial trade newspaper Women's Wear Daily (WWD) did publish information late in 1996 on apparel

TABLE 7.2. Average hourly apparel worker wages
(in U.S. dollars)

Country	Wages
Bangladesh	$.10–.16
Myanmar[a]	.10–.18
Pakistan	.21
Vietnam	.26
India	.26
Sri Lanka	.31
Indonesia	.34
China	.20–.68
Philippines	.94
Thailand	1.02
Haiti	.49
Nicaragua	.76
Mexico	1.08
Guatemala	1.25
Honduras	1.31
El Salvador	1.38
Dominican Republic	1.62
Jamaica	1.80
Costa Rica	2.38

[a] Listed as Burma in *WWD*.
Sources: "Labor Costs: Where and How Much?" *Women's Wear Daily*, December 31, 1996. Accessed at ⟨http://www.nlsearch.com⟩, 8/12/99; United Nations Development Programme, *Human Development Report, 1999*, Table 4, pp. 148–50.

worker wages per hour. Included were the nineteen relatively poor countries of Asia and Latin America listed in Table 7.2. Unfortunately, no information was provided for countries in the Middle East or Africa. Even so, the data amply testify to the prevalence of low wages in the industry. They also strongly indicate that in

Asia wage rates were substantially below the levels in Latin America. The unweighted country mean wage in Asia was about $0.44 per hour, that in Latin America about $1.34.

The question that arises is why the labor force in Latin American and particularly in Asia would work for the very low wage rates reported by *WWD*. In economic theory, wages fall within a range limited by the marginal productivity of labor at the high end and the wages offered by the next best alternative available to workers at the low end. Employers will not pay workers more than what the last worker hired contributes to the firm's revenue, and employees will not accept wages lower than they could secure in alternative employment. The actual wage rate paid within that range depends upon the relative bargaining strength of the two sides.

The employment alternatives available to workers are in large part determined by their country's level of economic development. In the countries under consideration here, none – with the possible exception of Jamaica – has experienced the kind of structural transformation that characterizes economic modernization. Unlike economically developed countries where the percentage of the labor force employed in agriculture typically is around 5 percent, in this group of countries that percentage is much higher. For the Asian countries, the labor force in agriculture ranges from China's 72 percent to Sri Lanka's 35 percent. In Latin America the range, excepting Jamaica, is from 67 percent for Haiti, to 20 percent for Costa Rica. Asia's weighted mean agricultural labor force comes to about two-thirds of the employed work force; in Latin America the proportion is about one-third (Table 7.3).

What makes the continued role of agriculture significant is that almost everywhere the agriculture sector tends to experience low relative levels of labor productivity. Compared to the rest of the economy, output per worker is low. As a result, incomes in this sector also are lower than those in the rest of the economy.

TABLE 7.3. Percentage of labor force in agriculture, agriculture as percentage of gross domestic product (GDP), and relative labor productivity of agriculture for selected countries by region

Country	Percentage of Labor in Agriculture	Agriculture as Percentage of GDP	Relative Labor Productivity
Bangladesh	63	24	.38
Myanmar	73	59	.81
Pakistan	50	25	.50
Vietnam	62	26	.42
India	71	25	.35
Sri Lanka	35	22	.63
Indonesia	39	16	.41
China	72	19	.26
Philippines	37	19	.51
Thailand	58	11	.19
UNWEIGHTED MEAN	56	25	.45
WEIGHTED MEAN[a]	67	22	.33
Haiti	68	30	.44
Nicaragua	28	34	1.21
Mexico	28	5	.18
Guatemala	51	24	.47
Honduras	46	20	.43
El Salvador	35	13	.37
Dominican Republic	24	12	.50
Jamaica	7	8	1.14
Costa Rica	20	15	.75
UNWEIGHTED MEAN	34	18	.53
WEIGHTED MEAN[a]	31	10	.32

[a] Weighted by labor force.

Source: World Bank, *World Development Indicators, 1999* (Washington, DC: World Bank, 1999): Labor force calculated from Tables 2.3 and 2.4; agriculture's share of GDP, Table 4.2; relative productivity weights, Tables 2.33 and 4.2.

Table 7.3 illustrates this phenomenon. In the table, agriculture's relative labor productivity for each country is obtained by dividing agriculture's percentage of total output by the percentage of the labor force working in that sector. If agriculture's share of production exceeds its share of the labor force, then its productivity compared to that of the rest of the economy is relatively high. The converse is that if the share of output is lower than the percentage of the labor force, agriculture's relative productivity is low. What Table 7.3 makes clear is that, with the exception of Nicaragua and Jamaica, labor productivity in agriculture everywhere is relatively low.

Taken together this means that work in agriculture in these societies pays low wages but that, particularly in Asia, this sector is responsible for most of the employment opportunities available to workers. That in turn means that to recruit a labor force the clothing industry has only to offer a somewhat higher wage than the very low one paid in agriculture. The strength of this mechanism is greater in Asia than elsewhere because agriculture there still is the dominant source of employment, in contrast to its diminished role in, for example, Central America (Table 7.4). Thus as Michael Piore has put it, the wages that are paid in the third world, though "deemed extortionate by Western standards, are not necessarily so from the perspective of the people who earn them abroad" (Piore 1997, 135).

The tendency for the clothing industry to pay its workers only slightly more than agriculture pays might have been at least partially offset if clothing workers had been able to engage in collective bargaining. But for the most part, union representation is absent in the apparel industry. In this industry, according to the ILO, "Today many workers fail to engage in collective bargaining because there is no recognized trade union at their place of work" (International Labour Organization 1996, 107). Because of this, clothing workers have not had access to the market power that

TABLE 7.4. Employment growth in clothing, changes in earnings in clothing, and purchasing power parity (PPP) gross national product (GNP) per capita, 1980–92

Country	Increase in Employment	Percentage Increase in Employment	Percentage Change in Wages	PPP GNP per Capita
Bangladesh	53,970	1,623.8	−3.6	1090
India	43,855	86.0	−3.6	1660
Sri Lanka	67,183	450.5	82.1	2460
Indonesia	113,884	734.7	112.0	3390
China	58,000	35.8	23.0	3070
Philippines	103,233	93.0	83.0	3670
Thailand	127,300	127.3	83.1	6490
Mexico	−4,568	−14.0	1.8	8110
Guatemala	1,521	38.0	−21.6	4060
Honduras	1,195	97.4	−36.0	2260
Jamaica	8,862	184.2	−31.8	3330
Costa Rica	12,494	75.5	−37.2	6510

Sources: Increase in Employment: International Labor Organization 1996, Table 3.3 ILO; Percentage Change in Wages: International Labour Organization 1996, Table 5.1; PPP GNP Per Capita: World Bank, World Tables 1999, Table 1.1.

unionization can provide. In the absence of organized labor, individual workers must secure work essentially as price takers. They either accept the going wage or seek work elsewhere. Thus the clothing industry has been able to secure its labor force at very low wages.

While the absence of high-paying alternatives and union representation explain low wages in the apparel industry, a mixed picture emerges for the movement of those wages over time. As reported in Table 7.4, wages increased substantially during the 1980s and early 1990s in Indonesia, the Philippines, Thailand,

and Sri Lanka, and they declined dramatically in Costa Rica, Honduras, Jamaica, and Guatemala. In other countries, such as Bangladesh, India, China, and Mexico, wages moved little.

In general, it appears that the experience in the Central American apparel industry with regard to the movement of wages has been much worse than that in Asia. But because of its scale, the pattern in Asia typifies the industry experience. In that region, wages fell only in the least-developed countries, Bangladesh and India. In the other Asian countries, at higher levels of economic development, wages increased, though remaining at low levels.

This suggests that while the clothing industry sought out low-cost labor, it did so mainly by relocating to Asia, and that the movement in the wages it paid over time depended upon the labor market context in which it found itself. What seems to have happened in the relatively developed countries of Asia is that the price of labor was bid up in clothing because wages were rising in other sectors of the economy as the process of growth proceeded. In India and Bangladesh, where low-wage agriculture remained predominant, that process did not occur. In short, the clothing industry was attracted to low-wage labor markets, but the trend in the wages it offered over time was determined by the alternative employment options created in the development process.

This all means that if the student anti-sweatshop movement is to mount a campaign that has real long-term hope of raising the living conditions of impoverished clothing workers, it will have to accept that there is more to the problem than entrepreneurial greed. Wages are lowest where worker alternatives are most limited. Growing employment in clothing does not always result in rising wages, but the chances of its doing so are greatest when that expansion occurs in a country where economic development is proceeding. When development occurs, wages in clothing rise because opportunities elsewhere grow. What students therefore should advocate is increased exports from poor nations and, in the context of that increase, the right of workers to form and join unions. That would give all workers, those in textiles as well as others, the enhanced bargaining power that enables them to secure increased wages.

ASSESSING THE STUDENT MOVEMENT

The strategy of the student movement is to seek alliances in the third world with "worker-allied groups – local NGOs, unions, and other organizations with knowledge of working conditions and established relationships with workers" – that have demonstrated "commitment to the needs and sensitivities of workers in a given situation" (Worker Rights Consortium 2000a, 5). In this effort it adopted a position consistent with recent left theorizing. Thus John Cavanagh, an activist in the anti-sweatshop movement, writes that "today governments are more compromised than ever in succumbing to corporate demands, and trade union movements around the world are much weaker." With that the case, the power to counter the strength of multinational corporations requires "new coalitions of citizen movements coordinating not only across labor, environmental, consumer and other social sectors, but also across geographic borders" (Cavanagh 1997, 40). That is precisely the strategy embodied in the WRC. It hopes to provide a vehicle to assist NGOs at the local level. They, in turn, are to provide third world workers with a way to bargain collectively on their own behalf.

There is plausibility to what Cavanagh has to say. Focusing international attention on working conditions in poor countries certainly is a means of dramatizing the needs of the poor. Furthermore, the students have avoided the self-defeating pitfall of advocating consumer boycotts and the banning of imports (Featherstone and Henwood 2001, 29).

Unfortunately, what the WRC possesses is more an aspiration for change than a strategy that can be successfully implemented. The WRC itself acknowledges that it has not assembled the network of NGOs essential to the task that it has envisioned, much less assessed whether those NGOs have the capacity to effectuate the transformation in labor relations that the WRC seeks. In a companion document to its main text, the WRC repeats its commitment to mobilizing NGOs, but it mentions only two such organizations in Central America, without providing any further information concerning their size or organizational capability. The only other NGO specifically cited is Labor Rights in China. But since that organization lacks a physical presence in the country, it is not able, at least at present, to implement the role the WRC envisions for it. In tacit recognition of the weakness in its roster of organizations for the implementation of its strategy, the WRC notes that it "will continue to draw on the expertise of its Advisory Council member in extending the NGO network" (Worker Rights Consortium 2000b, 3).

The WRC faces a future of great uncertainty. It does not possess the infrastructure necessary for the implementation of its strategy, and it is far from clear that it ever will. Given its organizational resources, it is likely that the best the WRC will be able to do is mobilize NGOs on a very limited, localized basis. Anything else is almost certainly beyond the WRC's capacity. Notwithstanding the WRC's confrontational stance, it is hard to see how the organization either at present or in the future will be able to have much impact on wages and working conditions in the global apparel industry.

That United Students Against Sweatshops (USAS) actively participated in the 1999 demonstrations in Seattle in opposition to the WTO is symbolic of another problem. Instead of seeing trade liberalization as a vehicle for job creation in poor nations, USAS, in a press release issued at the Seattle demonstrations, argued that the

WTO's "globalization policies . . . have resulted in a world of sky-rocketing income disparity, falling wages and massive environmental destruction" (United Students Against Sweatshops 1999, 1). USAS participation in the Seattle demonstrations gives the impression that the student movement does not recognize the contradiction involved in its doing so. On the one hand, USAS refuses to boycott apparel made in "sweatshops" because to do so would harm the workers employed in them. On the other hand, it opposes the WTO, the international body responsible for opening markets to the output of third world workers.

Yet the student demand that workers in the apparel industry be accorded the right to bargain collectively is valid. This is especially so since the right to unrestricted migration is not available to workers, but the new technology makes geographic relocation increasingly feasible for producers. Firms can take their production facilities and jobs wherever they choose, but labor is restricted in its ability to exercise a comparable mobility in seeking employment. This asymmetry in globalization means that workers deal with management from an increasingly weak position. As a consequence, their incomes rise less than they would if workers were free to seek employment without limit, and the ability of workers to avoid employment in sweatshop conditions is similarly damaged.

Unionization can provide workers with the countervailing power necessary for them to achieve greater equity in labor-management relations. Collective bargaining would make workers better able to secure for themselves the advances in income levels and health and safety conditions that economic growth permits. Standing in the way of unionization, of course, is the strong vested interest factory owners possess in resisting enhanced worker bargaining power. Avoiding collective bargaining and instead dealing with individual workers one at a time maximizes management's bargaining leverage in dealing with its labor force. In this way, businesses act in the interest of keeping production costs as low as possible.

The effort by management to deprive its labor force of parity in negotiations is what makes the WRC's task frustratingly difficult. Indeed, as things stand at present, that task is almost certainly beyond the reach of the WRC. The leverage over management likely to be generated by local NGOs and their allies cannot match the capability of businesses to resist. With the labor markets in poor countries characterized by limited alternatives for workers, and with the option of relocating available to producers, it is hard to envision that the coalition conceived by the WRC could, on any but an episodic basis, pressure firms to accept collective bargaining (Massing 2001, 5–6).

What would help unions gain a foothold in an industry like global apparel is an enforceable international code protecting workers' right to form unions and engage in collective bargaining. Without that, the labor-management relationship is too one-sided for standard labor organizing strategies, or even for efforts like those of the WRC, to have much impact. An international agreement on union rights is needed as well as the establishment of international machinery to ensure compliance – a labor counterpart to the WTO, promoting workers' rights as the WTO promotes global trade.

Such an international labor code would not set levels of wages or working conditions. A code to ensure the right of unions to exist is not the same as dictating the outcome of the negotiating process. Thus such a code would not be vulnerable to the charge that it represents a hidden form of protection for the industries of the developed world. It could be defended in the name of achieving harmonization in labor relations, and as such, it would be impervious to the objection that it provided an advantage for one group of countries over another.

Nevertheless, the effective implementation of such a code would mean in all likelihood that in an industry such as apparel wages would settle at a higher level than they are at present, though still within a range dictated by the local labor market. Similarly, it is probable that collective bargaining would produce advances in work environments and a reduction in sweatshop conditions. Especially in the context of economic growth and an increasing demand for labor, collective bargaining protected by an international authority holds out the promise of improved standards of living, particularly for workers like those who have attracted the attention of the student movement.

It does not seem far-fetched to hope that social activists such as those in the student anti-sweatshop movement might adopt this goal as fundamental to their agenda. Precisely because markets, including labor markets, have been internationalized, advocates of labor rights will have to adopt a strategy that itself operates at the global level. Failing this, workers will find themselves without the tools to bargain successfully with firms that have, on a worldwide scale, both access to resources and the potential to relocate.

As I argued earlier, the obvious candidate among existing international organizations to administer such a labor and union rights regime would be a much enhanced and empowered ILO. The ILO is a United Nations organization in which each country delegation is composed of representatives of business, labor, and the government. At present there are 174 member states. Of the 176 "conventions" that have been passed by the ILO since its inception in 1919, 7 have come to be recognized as "core labor standards." Two of these conventions specifically address the right to organize and bargain collectively. The first was accepted by the ILO in 1948, and the second was adopted in 1949 (International Confederation of Free Trade Unions 1999, 1–2).

These two conventions set a standard to which all countries can be held accountable. The first, the Convention on the Freedom of Association and Protection of the Right to Organize (C87), is very detailed in specifying that all workers have the right to belong to organizations of their own choosing, that they have the right to set their own rules and select their own leaders, and that their organizations should not be vulnerable to either government interference or government efforts to disband a functioning union. The second, the Convention on the Right to Organize and Collective Bargaining (C98), protects individual workers from anti-union discrimination in both hiring and dismissal. In addition, it stipulates that employers are not permitted to establish nominal unions that in reality are under their control. Collective bargaining is explicitly endorsed. This convention calls on countries to take measures "to encourage and promote the full development and utilisation of machinery for voluntary negotiation between employers and workers' organizations, with a view to the regulation of terms and conditions of employment by means of collective agreements" (International Labour Organization 2000).

Its enforcement and monitoring capabilities must be greatly strengthened if the ILO is to successfully supervise the global growth of union representation. The organization already possesses oversight mechanisms. But these are by no means strong enough for the ILO to act as a labor rights counterpart to the WTO. This weakness is particularly true for conventions that, though passed by the organization, have not been ratified by all the individual countries. In those cases, the abstaining country can claim to be exempt from even the limited enforcement that the ILO is capable of implementing.

The fact that neither convention on trade union rights has been ratified by the United States could provide a student movement intent on achieving global labor rights with a potentially fruitful organizing opportunity. The student movement could direct its efforts on behalf of global workers toward organizing supporters to pressure the United States into accepting these two conventions.

Such a strategy would give the student movement a domestic presence with opportunities for growth, opportunities that are not present when it focuses on overseas monitoring. At the same time, ratification of these conventions by the United States would be a valuable first step in a strategy to achieve a worldwide enforcement and monitoring system for labor rights. Acceptance by the United States of the right of all workers to bargain collectively would go far toward making globalization a more just process than it is at present.

Successful union organizing in industries like clothing needs a globally enforced code of conduct covering union rights. Students can be important contributors to the acceptance and implementation of such a code. But they will have to shift their sights and endorse the global. Just as trade advocates fought for the WTO, and investors attempted to secure the MAI, to achieve their goals supporters of workers' rights will have to struggle on behalf of international rules governing the rights of labor.

EIGHT

Saving Globalization

The United States, far more than any other country, has had a decisive voice in determining the content of the policies and procedures that have accompanied globalization. Its voice has been and still is dominant in multilateral organizations such as the World Bank and the IMF, and it was the most powerful influence in shaping the content of the rules that the WTO enforces (Mandle 2001).

In all of this, the position of the United States has been remarkably consistent over the years. The transition from Republican administrations in the 1980s to Democratic ones in the 1990s resulted in no change in fundamentals and the same is likely to be true of the administration of George W. Bush. The economist John Williamson is given credit for first labeling as "the Washington Consensus" the package of policies endorsed by the United States. With the Washington Consensus, the United States exercised pressure on other nations to emphasize markets and diminish the role of the public sector. As Williamson formulated it, the Washington Consensus included ten elements (Williamson 1999, 2):

1. Fiscal discipline in government spending.
2. A redirection of public expenditures away from subsidies and toward education, health, and infrastructure.
3. A reduction of marginal tax rates.
4. Decontrol of interest rates.
5. Movement away from fixed exchange rates to more market determined ones.
6. Trade liberalization.
7. Liberalization of foreign direct investment inflows.
8. Privatization of public enterprises.
9. Deregulation of output markets.
10. Securing of private property rights.

The policy orientation of the Washington Consensus is thus unmistakable. Its intention is to advance the role of markets at the expense of other social institutions.

In some respects the Washington Consensus has worked well. Policies to free FDI, for example, do seem to have helped at least some countries to accelerate their economic growth. And the liberalization of trade has advanced the interests of consumers throughout the world as flows of imports and exports have increased dramatically in recent years. But the reduction in the role of government that the Consensus has been interpreted to call for does not work well in all contexts. As we have seen, this certainly is true for international financial markets. Furthermore, in its commitment to reduce the public sector, the advocates of the Consensus typically pay inadequate attention to the dislocations that globalization causes. Building strong safety nets to protect the interests of displaced workers is not included in the agenda. In this and other areas, the Washington Consensus is in need of reversal.

It is not too late to reform globalization. The institutions associated with it are still under construction, and it is therefore possible to reduce the one-sidedness of the process. Because the technology that created market integration is relatively new, the rules and structures that will govern the emerging international economic system remain embryonic. What is clear even now, however, is that in globalization, as in all market systems, mechanisms to adjudicate conflicting claims are needed, as are the means to monitor and adjust the system. It is this last – the desirability of reshaping globalization to make it as fair as possible – that has been the concern of this study.

For the most part, anti-global activists do not view multinational negotiations as a satisfactory vehicle for reforming the global economy and making it more equitable. Only among some of those who want to reform global financial markets is there recognition that changes will require agreements among the governments of sovereign states. Unfortunately, the student anti-sweatshop movement, among others, has failed to see that improved working conditions for employees require a global codification of labor rights. And, of course, the supporters of localism reject globalization altogether.

Similarly indifferent to the desirability of international negotiations are those who favor the United States' using the threat of trade sanctions to reform the global economy. The difficulty here is that this call for America to remodel globalization is a call to refashion precisely the system that the United States has – more than any other nation – created. Jeff Faux makes this explicit, though he does not recognize the irony of his own advocacy of U.S. unilateralism:

> If the essential notion of the Washington consensus is to export the American economic model to the rest of the world, why not export all of it – not just accounting rules, but the whole package of a mixed economy in which nonmarket values such as the dignity of labor, ecological balance, and democratic community have enforceable claims? (Faux 1999, 6)

As we have seen, what advocates of this position would have the United States do is include labor, human rights, and environmental standards in all future trade agreements with the country. Failure to adhere to such standards would put a country at risk of United States-imposed trade sanctions.

It is highly doubtful that in the near future the values of, as Faux puts it, the mixed economy will become as important to United States policy makers as is their support for free markets. But even if that were to happen and the United States wanted to "export" a refurbished American economic model, it is difficult to envision how such a strategy of American unilateralism could be implemented. It is one thing to watch a country deregulate its markets. It is quite another to observe and monitor the implementation of market regulations, labor rights, environmental controls, and support mechanisms. Attempting to do all of this would require a monumental job of world policing; its complexities would make such a process vast and expensive. No less difficult would be the task of determining the level and nature of the sanctions to be imposed on transgressors. It is not difficult to envision the merciless lobbying that would occur within the United States by real or potential victims of country violators. There would be a very real risk that policing would become a vehicle for protecting the most effective domestic lobbies rather than for securing global justice.

A less radical version of unilateralism has been suggested by William Greider. In his proposal, the onus of reform would fall on American-based corporations and thus would not require the United States to tell other countries what to do. He writes that "since it is obvious that the WTO and other international forums have no intention of acting, Americans really have no moral choice but to assert responsibility." The way he would have this done is for the United States to pass domestic legislation imposing rules on the behavior of America-based multinational corporations.

Such legislation would require, at least at first, only that firms provide information on where and how production is undertaken – this in order to empower workers and other activists. A firm's failure to provide such information would be met by tariff penalties on its accessing the American market. In acknowledging that such disclosure requirements are modest at best, Greider accurately points out that they must be so in order "not to stymie industrial development in low-wage economies or to rewrite laws for other societies." Nevertheless, Greider's hope is that laws requiring companies to provide such information "can set the stage for subsequent legislation that eventually establishes minimum standards for corporate behavior on environment protection, labor issues and human rights" (Greider 2000, 12).

Notwithstanding the seeming reasonableness of his suggestion, Greider's proposal for disclosure underscores the limits of U.S. unilateralism. For the fact remains that most multinational corporations are not based in the United States. Data compiled by the United Nations indicate that, in 1997, 27 of the 100 largest multinational corporations were based in the United States; 45 found their home in the EU; 17 were in Japan; 3 in Canada; and the remainder scattered in Australia, New Zealand, South Korea, Switzerland, and Venezuela (United Nations Conference on Trade and Development 1999, 82) Greider's idea, even if implemented, would leave untouched most of the multinational corporations active in the global economy. At best, therefore, his is a partial approach to solving a problem that is beyond the reach of even as powerful a country as the United States.

No single country can be expected to create rules that adequately take into account the vast array of circumstances existing among the nations of the world. In any case, the kind of unilateralism suggested by both Faux and Greider really does not address the basic problem caused by globalization: the damage that is done to some as a result of change that is beneficial to most. Job loss and industry decline are caused by the same process that creates employment and raises income. Because of this the focus should be on ameliorating the injuries that such change inflicts on innocent victims.

The crisis in the Caribbean over the future of its banana industry illustrates both the problem and the way forward (the following two paragraphs are based on Mandle 2000). In 1993 economic integration resulted in the creation of a single European market. With that, the British no longer were able to protect banana producers in the Caribbean, as they had in the past. After a period of very difficult negotiations the members of the European Union agreed on a banana marketing system that continued to protect both the industry in the Caribbean and the firms that marketed that region's produce. However, the American firm Chiquita protested that the scheme discriminated against its interests and prevailed upon the Clinton administration to take the case before the WTO. There, the United States position was endorsed, and the European banana marketing regime was declared to be in violation of the non-discrimination rules that govern international trade.

The problem is that the WTO decision on bananas threatens to create a major social crisis in the Caribbean. This is because the costs of banana production in the region are far higher than elsewhere, and as a result, the industry's profitability is dependent upon tariff protection. Analysts at the British anti-poverty organization Oxfam are not alone in worrying that "the loss of the banana trade with the EU would lead to mass poverty, and high levels of unemployment and instability in the region" (Godfrey 1998, 7). The magnitude of the threat derives from the economic importance of the banana industry, particularly for the Windward Island nations of Dominica, Grenada, St. Lucia, St. Vincent, and the Grenadines, which can scarcely be exaggerated. Even today, after a considerable downturn experienced by the industry during the 1990s, bananas take up almost one-third of the arable land in these four countries and alone are responsible for 43 percent of the exports and 21 percent of the gross domestic products of those countries. The potential dislocation that would result if the banana industry were to crumble, with nothing to replace it, would be especially devastating and unjust because the producers in the industry are peasants with little or no margin for economic loss. The raw edge of globalization is as clear in this example as it can be: at the behest of a multinational corporation, hard-working but poor peasants would be driven to penury.

What is important here is that the banana problem is not atypical. As market integration proceeds, the restructuring of patterns of production inevitably occurs. High-cost producers, such as the Caribbean banana growers, will face bankruptcy as they confront competitors whose costs are lower or who produce higher quality output. The issue is not whether such injuries will occur, but what to do about them when they do happen.

To make the process both efficient and fair, producers should be assisted in making the transition to industries in which they can competitively hold their own. Much of the burden in this will inevitably have to be borne by national governments. But precisely because globalization is global and the benefits of the process spread internationally, there is as well an argument to be made for assistance to be provided by the international community, particularly by the developed nations. Such aid can be provided on both the demand and the supply side of markets.

The argument is, therefore, that while the United States should not assume total responsibility for the content of globalization, it can and should participate in the process of making the emerging global economy more equitable. Fundamental to this participation is its abandoning its zeal for reducing the role for government in the economy. Instead, it must recognize that providing both domestic and international support for workers dislocated by the process is essential if globalization is to be just. In addition, as I have argued, the global economy would be more equitable if union-organizing rights were codified and enforced worldwide. The United States could take the lead in multilateral negotiations to secure such an agreement. And, as I have also noted, the whole system could be made more stable if financial flows were constrained with a mechanism such as the Tobin Tax, a position that the United States similarly could advance in multilateral forums.

Above and beyond these positions, there is probably no more important contribution that the United States could make than to adhere to its widely proclaimed belief in open markets (Sanger 2001). Today, not only in the United States but in the European Union as well, non-tariff barriers to imports remain critical in restricting the growth of poor countries. Thus the ambassador to the United Nations from Antigua and Barbuda reasonably points to the hypocrisy of the developed countries' insisting on "the principle of free trade for the developing world and an exemption of the same for the industrialized countries" (*Caribbean Daylight* 2000).

On this, Jeffrey J. Schott has noted that though the market in the United States is more open than those in most other countries, nevertheless, "there are a few notable barriers whose reductions would have significant consequences." Schott identifies three such areas: tariffs on textile and clothing imports; quotas applied to agricultural imports; and the use of anti-dumping legislation in the United States as an instrument for banning the importing of man-ufactured goods. Schott's view is that liberalization in these areas would be in America's national interest. It would enhance this country's ability to negotiate trade concessions. At the same time, the increased availability of imports would both widen the choices available to consumers and put downward pressure on the prices they had to pay (Schott 2000, 14).

More to the point, liberalization in these areas would also be of great significance to poor nations. Agricultural subsidies to domestic producers place overseas farmers at a competitive disadvantage, quotas on sugar imports frustrate the production efforts of tropical nations capable of supplying the United States market, and domestic content requirements for textiles limit third world exports of apparel to America.[1] If the United States would further open its market, many third world textile and agricultural producers would be able to increase their sales without much delay. This, of course, would have immediate consequences for income and employment in poor countries.

In addition to opening their markets, the developed countries could contribute to an acceleration of third world economic growth by helping to refocus the development of new technologies to the needs of poor countries. As Sachs has noted, at present efforts to generate new technologies are "overwhelmingly directed at rich-country problems." New technologies frequently are not geographically neutral in their applicability. Many of them do not easily cross what Sachs has called "the ecological divide." Especially in agriculture, where climate and soil differences are critical to the successful application of new methods of production, research and development must be environmentally specific. According to Sachs, that there is a "profound imbalance in the global production of knowledge . . . probably [is] the most powerful engine of divergence in global well-being between the rich and the poor" (Sachs 1999, 4).

To turn again to the example of bananas, the United States could assist Caribbean nations in at least three areas. First, the

---

[1] For example, the African Trade and Development Act of 2000 limits duty-free imports of apparel from Africa to products made with United States yarn and United States fabric unless such yarn and fabric are not available in the country. The United States limits sugar imports by imposing country-by-country import quotas.

country could provide financial assistance for research in the region aimed at achieving greater competitiveness for the Caribbean banana industry in world markets. Second, it could help in the effort to identify alternative industries that might emerge as bananas recede in relative importance. Finally, having identified new regional industries, the United States could help pay for the worker and management retraining necessary for those industries to become commercially successful.

Thus there is an almost perfect parallel between what is required domestically and what is needed internationally to make globalization more just. In both instances the task should not be to impede structural transformation. Nor is it necessary for rich countries to impose their will on poor ones. Rather the problem is to identify what in the globalization process inflicts unjust harm and then move to minimize that damage. Specifically, policies are needed to reduce the costs of the transitions that globalization sets in motion. In countries like the United States this involves policies supportive of workers and firms dislocated by trade liberalization. In the poor countries, in addition, the restructuring itself will need to be facilitated. This can be done with assistance by the developed world both in market access and in the development of new techniques of production.

It is possible to envision a global politics to make globalization more equitable. Many of the participants in the anti-globalization movement can and should find a place in such an effort. After all, at root it is a concern for justice and equity that animates the anti-globalization demonstrators. But, as we have seen, strong unilateralist and anti-modernist attitudes dominate that movement. Mistakenly seen by activists as advancing the interests of the world's disadvantaged population, their current positions are in reality at cross-purposes with the interests of the poor. Above all, the poor need development, accompanied by domestic and international policies of amelioration and including the global recognition of union rights. Most activists have failed to perceive the need for both elements of this package – economic growth and fairness. Though a change in their perception is not inconceivable, at the moment it does seem improbable.

Nonetheless, some in the movement seem to be aware of the problem. Jim Phillips, in an article in *Dollars and Sense* in the aftermath of the Seattle demonstrations, wrote that "the unity among WTO opponents in this country . . . takes on a more ominous aspect in the eyes of some Third World observers" who believe that the labor/environmental/human rights coalition was "motivated by a fear of competition with the third world." Phillips, for example, recognizes that the position adopted by the United Steel Workers in favor of anti-dumping legislation that protects American markets from low-priced imports is "deeply resented by industries in many developing countries." Similarly, he reports that the issue of environmental protection raises the danger of a north-south divide, in which agreements to protect endangered species generate fear in poor countries that enforcing the agreements would slow economic growth (Phillips 2000, 30, 31).

Even Phillips, however, gives no indication that he appreciates the fundamental change in attitude that is required among activists in order to align the movement with the interests of the global poor. Globalization's ability to facilitate industrial development, and thus to help reduce poverty in places by-passed in the past by that process, is a touchstone that must guide policies in this sphere. Only with that as a guide do the complementary policies that can achieve fairness make sense. In turn, those policies of support can be operationalized best through multilateral agreement, not by U.S. dictation. Unfortunately, none of this is present in Phillips's discussion (Phillips 2000, 30–32).

It is true that growth alone does not secure justice. But it is certainly also true that the alleviation of poverty cannot be accomplished without growth (Dollar and Kraay 2000). Real solidarity with the poor requires a recognition that justice and growth both are possible and necessary. Nothing would be more valuable for achieving a just globalization than for activists to move to such a recognition.

References

ONE. INTRODUCTION

Ehrenreich, Barbara. 2000. "Forward." In Sarah Anderson and John Cavanagh, with Thea Lee (eds.), *Field Guide to the Global Economy*. New York: New Press, ix–x.

Faux, Jeff. 1999. "Viewpoints: Slouching toward Seattle." ⟨http://www.epinet.org/webfeatures/viewpoints/slouch.html⟩. Accessed 3/5/00.

Fishlow, Albert, and Karen Parker. 1999. *Growing Apart: The Causes and Consequences of Global Wage Inequality*. New York: Council on Foreign Relations Press.

Nove, Alec. 1983. *The Economics of Feasible Socialism*. London: George Allen and Unwin.

Reich, Robert. 1999. "Whose Trade?" *Nation*. December 6, pp. 11–17.

Sachs, Wolfgang. 1996. "Introduction." *The Development Dictionary: A Guide to Knowledge As Power*. London and New Jersey: Zed Books.

TWO. ECONOMIC GLOBALIZATION AND THE DEVELOPMENT OF POOR NATIONS

Bhagwati, Jagdish. 1998. *A Stream of Windows: Unsettling Reflections on Trade, Immigration, and Democracy*. Cambridge, MA, and London: MIT Press.

Bordo, Michael D., Barry Eichengreen, and Douglas A. Irwin. 1999. "Is Globalization Today Really Different from Globalization a Hundred Years Ago?" In Susan M. Collins and Robert Z. Lawrence (eds.), *Brookings Trade Forum 1999*. Washington, DC: Brookings Institution Press, 1–72.

Coclanis, Peter A., and Tilak Doshi. 2000. "Globalization in Southeast Asia." In Louis Ferleger and Jay R. Mandle (eds.), "Dimensions of Globalization." *Annals of the American Academy of Political and Social Science*. Vol. 570 (July), 49–64.

Eckes, Alfred E., Jr. 1999. "U.S. Trade History." In William A. Lovett, Alred E. Eckes, Jr., and Richard L. Brinkman (eds.), *U.S. Trade Policy: History, Theory and the WTO*. Armonk, NY, and London: M. E. Sharpe, 51–105.

Friedman, Thomas L. 1999. *The Lexus and the Olive Tree: Understanding Globalization*. New York: Farrar, Straus and Giroux.

Krueger, Anne O. 1998. "Introduction." In Anne O. Krueger (ed.), *The WTO as an International Organization*. Chicago and London: University of Chicago Press.

Krueger, Anne O. 1995. *Trade Policies and Developing Nations*. Washington, DC: Brookings Institution.

O'Rourke, Kevin H., and Jeffrey G. Williamson. 1999. *Globalization and History: The Evolution of a Nineteenth-Century Atlantic Economy*. Cambridge, MA: MIT Press.

Stever, H. Guyford, and Janet H. Muroyama. 1988. "Overview." In Janet H. Huroyama and H. Guyford Stever (eds.), *Globalization of Technology: International Perspectives*. Washington, DC: National Academy Press, 1–11.

Uchitelle, Louis. 1998. "Some Economic Interplay Comes Nearly Full Circle." *New York Times on the Web*. April 30. ⟨http://nytimes.qpass.com⟩.

United Nations Development Programme. 1999. *Human Development Report 1999*. New York: Oxford University Press.

World Bank. 1998–99. *World Development Report 1998/99*. New York: Oxford University Press.

THREE. THE SOURCES OF OPPOSITION

Aaronson, Susan Ariel. 2001. *Taking Trade to the Streets: The Lost History of Public Efforts to Shape Globalization.* Ann Arbor: University of Michigan Press.

Bergsten, C. Fred. 1999. "Comments and Discussion." In Susan M. Collins and Robert Z. Lawrence (eds.), *Brookings Trade Forum 1999.* Washington, DC: Brookings Institution Press, 194–200.

Burtless, Gary, Robert Z. Lawrence, Robert E. Litan, and Robert J. Shapiro. 1998. *Globaphobia: Confronting Fears about Open Trade.* Washington, DC: Brookings Institution Press.

Chen, Kathy. 2002. "Lawmakers May Gain Most from Boost to Worker Aid." *Wall Street Journal Online.* May 24. ⟨www.online.wsj.com⟩. Accessed 5/25/02.

Cooper, Helen, Bob Davis, and Greg Hitt. 1999. "WTO's Failure in Bid to Launch Trade Talks Emboldens Protesters." *Wall Street Journal Interactive Edition.* December 6. ⟨http://www.interactive.wsj.com⟩. Accessed 12/14/99.

Dasgupta, S. A. Mody, S. Roy, and D. Wheeler. 1995. "Environmental Regulation and Development: A Cross Country Empirical Analysis." *World Bank Policy Research Department Working Paper No. 1448.* Washington, DC: World Bank.

Davis, Bob. 1999. "Trade Demonstrations Hurt Clinton Legacy, Gore Push." *Wall Street Journal Interactive Edition.* December 2. ⟨http://www.interactive.wsj.com⟩. Accessed 12/14/99.

Destler, I. M., and Peter J. Balint. 1999. *The New Politics of American Trade: Trade, Labor and the Environment.* Washington, DC: Institute for International Economics.

Eckes, Alfred E., Jr. 1999. "U.S. Trade History." In William A. Lovett, Alfred E. Eckes, Jr., and Richard L. Brinkman (eds.), *U.S. Trade Policy: History, Theory and the WTO.* Armonk, NY, London: M. E. Sharpe, 51–105.

Economic Report of the President. 2001. Washington, DC: Government Printing Office.

Economist. 1999. "A Global Disaster." December 11.

Fredriksson, Per G., and Daniel L. Millimet. 2000. "Is There a Race to the Bottom in Environmental Policies?" Paper presented at the North American Commission for Environmental Cooperation Symposium on Understanding the Linkages between Trade and Environment. Available at ⟨http://www.cec.org/Programs_Projects/Trade_Eniron_Econ/pdfs/fredrik. pdf⟩. Accessed 6/4/01.

Greider, William. 1999. "The Battle beyond Seattle." *Nation.* December 27. ⟨http://www.thenation.com⟩. Accessed 12/14/00.

Jackson, John H. 1998. "Designing and Implementing Effective Dispute Settlement Procedures: WTO Dispute Settlement, Appraisal and Prospects." In Anne O. Krueger (ed.), *The WTO as an International Organization.* Chicago and London: University of Chicago Press, 161–80.

Nation. 1999. "Democracy Bites the WTO." December 27. ⟨http://www.thenation.com⟩. Accessed 12/14/00.

Odell, John, and Barry Eichengreen. 1998. "The United States, the ITO, and the WTO: Exit Options, Agent Slack and Presidential Leadership." In Anne O. Krueger (ed.), *The WTO as an International Organization.* Chicago and London: University of Chicago Press, 181–209.

Ostry, Sylvia. 1999. "The Future of the World Trade Organization." In Susan M. Collins and Robert Z. Lawrence (eds.), *Brookings Trade Forum 1999.* Washington, DC: Brookings Institution Press, 167–90.

Rodrik, Dani. 1998. "Has Globalization Gone Too Far? An Interview with Dani Rodrik." *Challenge.* Vol. 41, no. 2 (March–April), 81–94.

Rodrik, Dani. 1997. *Has Globalization Gone Too Far?* Washington, DC: Institute for International Economics.

Scheve, Kenneth F., and Matthew J. Slaughter. 2001. *Globalization and the Perception of American Workers.* Washington, DC: Institute for International Economics.

Schott, Jeffrey. 2000. "The WTO after Seattle." In Jeffrey J. Schott (ed.), *The WTO after Seattle.* Washington, DC: Institute for International Economics, 3–40.

World Bank. 2000. "Assessing Globalization: Is Globalization Causing a 'Race to the Bottom' in Environmental Standards?" *Briefing Papers*. April. ⟨http://www.worldbank.org/html/extdr/pb/globalization/paper4.htm⟩. Accessed 6/4/01.

FOUR. ALTERNATIVES TO GLOBALIZATION

Associated Press. 1999. "WTO Negotiations End in Failure, but Talks May Continue in Geneva." *Wall Street Journal Interactive Edition.* December 4. ⟨http://www.interactive.wsj.com⟩. Accessed 12/14/99.

Bhagwati, Jagdish. 1998. *A Stream of Windows: Unsettling Reflections on Trade, Immigration, and Democracy.* Cambridge, MA, and London: MIT Press.

Borosage, Robert L. 2000. "Who Speaks for the Third World?" *The American Prospect.* Vol. 11, no. 5 (January 17). ⟨http://www.prospect.org⟩.

Fallows, James. 1997. "The Fallacy of Ango-American Economics." In Michael Lind (ed.), *Hamilton's Republic: Readings in the American Nationalist Tradition.* New York. Free Press, 310–16.

Faux, Jeff. 1998. "Jeff Faux Replies." *Dissent.* Spring, 81–83.

Faux, Jeff. 1996. *The Party's Not Over: A New Vision for the Democrats.* New York. Basic Books.

Golub, Stephen S. 1997. "International Labor Standards and International Trade." *IMF Working Paper.* Vol. 97, no. 37 (April).

Green Party. 2000. Platform. As ratified at the Green Party National Convention, available at ⟨http://www.gp.orgplatform/gpp2000.html⟩.

Greider, William. 2000. "Shopping till We Drop." *Nation.* April 10, pp. 11–15.

Greider, William. 1997. "Saving the Global Economy." *Nation.* December 15, pp. 11–16.

International Confederation of Free Trade Unions. 1999. "Internationally Recognized Core Labour Standards in the United States." *Report for the WTO General Council Review of the Trade Policies of the*

United States. World Trade Organization, Geneva, July 12 and 14. ⟨http://www.icftu.org/english/els.escl99wtousa.html⟩. Accessed 9/2/99.

International Forum on Globalization. 1999. "Beyond the WTO: Alternatives to Economic Globalization. A Preliminary Report." Available at ⟨http://www.ifg.org/beyondwto.html⟩.

Klein, Naomi. 2000. "The Vision Thing." *Nation*, July 10. Available at ⟨http://www.thenation.com/issue/000710/0710klein.shtml⟩.

Krugman, Paul. 2000. "Reckonings: Once and Again." *New York Times on the Web*. January 2. ⟨http://www.nytimes.com⟩. Accessed 1/8/00.

Levinson, Jerome. 1999. "Certifying International Worker Rights." *EPI Briefing Paper*. ⟨http://www.epinet.org/briefingpapers/levinson.html⟩. Accessed 10/19/99.

Lind, Michael. 1995. *The Next American Nation: The New Nationalism and the Fourth American Revolution*. New York: Free Press.

Mandle, Jay R. 1998. "The Problem with Thinking Locally: A Critique of the Sierra Club's *The Case against the Global Economy.*" *Boston Review*. Vol. 23, nos. 3–4 (Summer 1998), 52–55.

Mandle, Jay R. 1996. *Persistent Underdevelopment: Change and Economic Modernization in the West Indies*. New York: Gordon and Breach Publishers.

Nation. 1997. "Fast Track Backtrack." December 1, pp. 3–4.

Palley, Thomas L. 1998. *Plenty of Nothing: The Downsizing of the American Dream and the Case for Structural Keynesianism*. Princeton, NJ: Princeton University Press.

Pollack, Andrew. 2000. "130 Nations Agree on Safety Rules for Biotech Food." *New York Times on the Web*. January 30. ⟨http://www.nytimes.qpass.com-archives⟩. Accessed 1/31/00.

Rodrik, Dani. 1998. "Democracies Pay Higher Wages." *NBER Working Paper No. 6364*. January.

United Nations Development Programme. 1999. *Human Development Report 1999*. New York: Oxford University Press.

Winestock, Geoff. 2000. "Clinton Renews Call for Standards: WTO Issue Heat Up Forum Talks." *Wall Street Journal Interactive Edition.* January 31. ⟨http://interactive.wsj.com⟩. Accessed 1/31/00.

World Bank. 1987. *World Development Report 1987.* New York: Oxford University Press.

FIVE. THE ANTI-GLOBALIZATION MOVEMENT AND THE MULTILATERAL AGREEMENT ON INVESTMENT

Amsden, Alice H. and Takashi Hikino. 2000. "The Bark Is Worse than the Bite: New WTO Law and Late Industrialization." In Louis Ferleger and Jay R. Mandle (eds.), "Dimensions of Globalization." *Annals of the American Academy of Social and Political Science.* Vol. 570 (July), 104–25.

Barlow, Maude, and Tony Clarke. 1998. *The Multilateral Agreement on Investment and the Threat to American Freedom.* New York: Stoddart.

Brewer, Thomas L., and Stephen Young. 1996. "Investment Policies in Multilateral and Regional Agreements: A Comparative Analysis." *Transnational Corporations.* Vol. 5, no. 1 (April), pp. 12–28.

de Jonquieres, Guy. 1998. "Foreign Investment: Monster or Mouse." *Financial Times.* February 16. ⟨http://www.fot.com/index.htm⟩.

Destler, I. M., and Peter J. Balint. 1999. *The New Politics of American Trade: Trade, Labor and the Environment.* Washington, DC: Institute for International Economics.

Dunning, John H. 1997. *The Advent of Alliance Capitalism.* New York: United Nations University Press.

Eizenstat, Stuart, and Jeffrey Lang. 1998. "Remarks Following the OECD Meeting on MAI." Paris, France, February 17. ⟨http:/www.state.gov/ www/policy_remarks/1998/980217_eizen_mai.html⟩.

Graham, Edward M. 2000. *Fighting the Wrong Enemy: Antiglobal Activists and Multinational Enterprises.* Washington, DC: Institute for International Economics.

Graham, Edward M., and Paul R. Krugman. 1990. "Trade-Related Investment Measures." In Jeffrey J. Schott (ed.), *Completing the Uruguay Round: A Results-Oriented Approach to the GATT Trade Negotiations*. Washington, DC: Institute for International Economics, 147–63.

James, Jeffrey. 1999. *Globalization, Information Technology and Development*. New York: St. Martin's Press.

Johnston, Donald J. 1998. "The Case for MAI." Letter to the *Financial Times*, February 24. ⟨http://www.ft.com/index.htm⟩.

Johnston, Donald J. 1997. "Informal Consultation with NGOs on the MAI." October 27. ⟨http://www.oecd.org/daf/cmis/mai/sgngo.htm⟩.

Krueger, Anne O. 1998. "An Agenda for the WTO." In Anne O. Krueger (ed.), *The WTO as an International Organization*. Chicago: University of Chicago Press, 401–10.

Larson, Alan. 1998. "Testimony before the House International Relations Committee, Subcommittee on International Economic Policy and Trade." March 6. ⟨http://www.state.gov/www/policy_remarks/1998/980306_larson_mai.html⟩.

Larson, Alan P. 1997. "MAI Briefing for Non-OECD Countries." *State of Play of MAI Negotiations*. Paris, France, September 17. ⟨http://www.oecd.org/daf/cmis/mai/maindex.htm⟩.

Lawrence, Robert Z. 1997. "The World Trade and Investment System and Developing Countries." In John H. Dunning and Khalil A. Hamdani (eds.), *The New Globalism and Developing Countries*. New York: United Nations University Press, 51–77.

Lawrence, Robert Z., Albert Bressand, and Takatoshi Ito. 1996. *A Vision for the World Economy: Openness, Diversity and Cohesion*. Washington, DC: Brookings Institution Press.

Lizza, Ryan. 2000. "Silent Partners: The Man behind the Anti-Free Trade Revolt." *New Republic*. January 10, pp. 22–25.

McCulloch, Rachel. 1990. "Investment Policies in the GATT." *World Economy*. Vol. 13, no. 4, pp. 541–52.

Organisation for Economic Co-operation and Development (OECD). 1998. *The MAI Negotiating Text (as of 14 February 1998)*. Directorate for Financial, Fiscal and Enterprise Affairs.

Organisation for Economic Co-operation and Development (OECD). 1996. *Globalisation of Industry: Overview and Sector Reports.* Paris: Organisation for Economic Co-operation and Development.

Ostry, Sylvia. 1999. "The Future of the World Trade Organization." In Susan M. Collins and Robert Z. Lawrence (eds.), *Brookings Trade Forum 1999.* Washington, DC: Brookings Institution Press, 167–90.

Preamble Center. 1998. "Update on MAI Negotiations at the OECD." December 10. ⟨http://www.preamble.org/MAI/dec98update.htm⟩. Accessed 2/17/00.

Public Citizen. n.d. "Global Trade Watch: The MAI Shell Game." ⟨http://www.citizen.org/pctrade/Shell_Game/Cover.htm⟩. Accessed 2/17/00.

Roessler, Frieder. 1996. "Diverging Domestic Policies and Multilateral Trade Integration." In Jagdish Bhagwati and Robert E. Hudec (eds.), *Fair Trade and Harmonization: Prerequisites for Free Trade?* Cambridge, MA: MIT Press, Vol. 2, pp. 21–56.

United Nations. 1999. *World Investment Report: Foreign Direct Investment and the Challenge of Development.* New York: United Nations Publication.

Western Governors' Association. 1997. *Multilateral Agreement on Investment: Potential Effects on State and Local Government.* Denver, CO: Western Governors' Association.

Witherell, William H. 1995. "The OECD Multilateral Agreement on Investment." *Transnational Corporations.* Vol. 4, no. 2. (August), pp. 3–9.

World Bank. 1999. *World Development Indicators 1999.* Washington, DC: World Bank.

SIX. REGULATING INTERNATIONAL FINANCIAL MARKETS

Agosin, Manuel R. 1998. "Liberalize, but Discourage Short-Term Flows." In Isabelle Grunberg (ed.), *Perspectives on International Financial Liberalization.* New York: United National Development Programme, 1–6.

Bank for International Settlements. n.d. "Central Bank Survey of Foreign Exchange and Derivatives Market Activity in April 1998: Preliminary Global Data." Press release. Available at ⟨http://www.bis.org/⟩. Accessed 3/19/00.

Bhagwati, Jagdish. 1998. "The Capital Myth." *Foreign Affairs.* Vol. 77, no. 3 (May/June), 7–12.

Eatwell, John, and Lance Taylor. 2000. *Global Finance at Risk: The Case for International Regulation.* New York: New Press.

Economic Report of the President, February 2000. Washington, DC: Government Printing Office.

Economic Report of the President, February 1999. Available at ⟨http://www.wais.access.gpo.gov⟩. Accessed 3/1/00.

Economist. 1998. "Keeping the Hot Money Out." ⟨http://www.stern.nyu.edu/globalmacro/⟩. Accessed 7/8/98.

Eichengreen, Barry. 1999. *Toward a New International Financial Architecture: A Practical Post-Asia Agenda.* Washington, DC: Institute for International Economics.

Garten, Jeffrey E. 1998. "A Global Central Bank Would Keep Hand on World Economic Rudder." *Seattle Post-Imtellinger.* Vol. 12, no. 185 (September 24), Editorial Section, 1–3.

Guitian, Manuel. 1998. "The Challenge of Managing Global Capital Flows." *Finance and Development.* Vol. 35, no. 2 (June), 14–17.

International Monetary Fund Research Department Staff. 1997. "Capital Flow Sustainability and Speculative Currency Attacks." ⟨http://www.stern.nyu.edu/globalmacro/⟩. Accessed 7/8/98.

Kaul, Inge, Isabelle Grunberg, and Mahbub ul Haq. 1996. "Overview." In Mahbub ul Haq, Inge Kaul, and Isabelle Grunberg (eds.), *The Tobin Tax: Coping with Financial Volatility.* New York: Oxford University Press, 1–12.

Nadal-De Simone, Francisco, and Piritta Sorsa. 1999. "A Review of Capital Account Restrictions in Chile in the 1990s." *A Working Paper of the International Monetary Fund.* WP/99/52.

Rodrik, Dani. 1999. *The New Global Economy and Developing Countries: Making Openness Work*. Washington, DC: Overseas Development Council. Distributed by Johns Hopkins University Press.

Rogoff, Kenneth. 1999. "International Institutions for Reducing Global Financial Instability." ⟨http://www.wws.princeton.edu/~krogoff/ rogoff.pdf⟩.

Stiglitz, Joseph. 1998. "Sound Finance and Sustainable Development in Asia." Keynote address to the Asia Development Forum. Manila, The Philippines, March 12. ⟨http://www.stern.nyu.edu/globalmocro/⟩.

Taylor, Lance, and Pieper Ute. 1996. *Reconciling Economic Reform and Sustainable Human Development: Social Consequences of Neo-Liberalism*. New York: United Nations Development Programme.

White, William R. 2000. "What Have We Learned from Recent Financial Crises and Policy Responses?" *BIS Working Papers, No. 84*. Basel, Switzerland: Bank for International Settlements. Available at ⟨http://www.bis.org⟩. Accessed 3/3/00.

World Bank, 2000. *Global Economic Prospects and the Developing Countries*. Washington, DC: World Bank.

World Bank, 1998. *World Development Indicators 1998*. Washington, DC: World Bank.

SEVEN. THE STUDENT ANTI-SWEATSHOP MOVEMENT

Apparel Industry Partnership. 1999. "Frequently Asked Question about the Apparel Industry Partnership." ⟨http://www.lchr.org/sweatshop/ faq.htm⟩. Accessed 9/1/99.

Appelbaum, Richard P., and Edna Bonacich. 2000. "The Key Is Enhancing the Power of Workers." *Chronicle of Higher Education*. April 7, pp. B4–B5.

Appelbaum, Richard, and Peter Dreier. 1999. "The Campus Anti-Sweatshop Movement." *The American Prospect*. No. 46. (September–October), 71–78.

Bhagwati, Jagdish. 1998. *A Stream of Windows: Unsettling Reflections on Trade, Immigration, and Democracy.* Cambridge, MA and London: MIT Press.

Cavanagh, John. 1997. "The Global Resistance to Sweatshops." In Andrew Ross (ed.), *No Sweat: Fashion, Free Trade and the Rights of Garment Workers.* New York: Verso, 39–50.

Collegiate Code of Conduct. 1998. "The Collegiate Code of Conduct for CLC Licensees [November 30, 1998, Task Force Draft]. ⟨http://www.news.wisc.edu/misc/code.html⟩. Accessed 8/14/99.

Dobnik, Verena. 1998. "Employees Sign Sweatshop Pact." Associated Press. November 5. ⟨http://www.cleanclothes.org/codes/AIP-3.htm⟩. Accessed 8/14/99.

Fair Labor Association. 2000. "Welcome to the Fair Labor Association." ⟨http://www.fairlabor.org⟩. Accessed 12/25/00.

Featherstone, Liza. 2000. "The New Student Movement." *Nation.* May 15, pp. 11–18.

Featherstone, Liza, and Doug Henwood. 2001. "Clothes Encounters: Activists and Economists Clash over Sweatshops." *Lingua Franca.* Vol. 11, no. 2 (March), 26–33.

Greenhouse, Steven. 1999. "17 Colleges Join against Sweatshops." *New York Times on the Web.* March 16. ⟨http://graphics.nytimes.com/images/⟩. Accessed 8/15/99.

Greenhouse, Steven. 1998. "Plans to Curtail Sweatshops Rejected by Union." *New York Times.* November 5. ⟨http://www.cleanclothes.org/codes/AIP-3.htm⟩. Accessed 8/14/99.

International Confederation of Free Trade Unions. 1999. "Internationally Recognized Core Labour Standards in the United States." Report for the WTO General Council Review of the Trade Policies of the United States." ⟨http://www/icftu.org/english/els/escl99wtousa.html⟩. Accessed 9/2/99.

International Labour Organization. 2000. "International Labour Standards." ⟨http://www.ilo.org⟩.

International Labour Organization. 1996. *Globalization of the Footwear, Textiles and Clothing Industries.* Geneva: International Labour Organization.

Massing, Michael. 2001. "From Protest to Program." *The American Prospect*. Vol. 12, no. 12 (Summer), 2–7.

Piore, Michael. 1997. "The Economics of the Sweatshop." In Andrew Ross (ed.), *No Sweat: Fashion, Free Trade and the Rights of Garment Workers*. New York: Verso, 135–42.

Ross, Andrew. 1997. "Introduction." In Andrew Ross (ed.), *No Sweat: Fashion, Free Trade and the Rights of Garment Workers*. New York: Verso, 9–37.

Sassen, Saskia. 2000. "Regulating Immigration in a Global Age: A New Policy Landscape." In Louis Ferleger and Jay R. Mandle (eds.), "Dimensions of Globalization." *Annals of the American Academy of Political and Social Science*. Vol. 570, (July), 65–77.

Singer, Sally. 1997. "Rat-Catching: An Interview with Bud Konheim." In Andrew Ross (ed.), *No Sweat: Fashion, Free Trade and the Rights of Garment Workers*. New York. Verso.

UNITE. n.d. *A UNITE Report on Campus Caps Made by BJ&B in the Dominican Republic*. ⟨http://www.uniteunion.org/sweatshops/schoocap.html⟩. Accessed 8/14/99.

United Nations Development Programme. 1999. *Human Development Report 1999*. New York: United Nations.

U.S. Census Bureau. 2000. *Statistical Abstract of the United States: 2000*. Washington, DC: Government Printing Office.

United Students Against Sweatshops. 1999. "United Students Against Sweatshops Position Paper on World Trade Organization, Seattle Round of Talks." ⟨http://www.umich.edu/~sole/usas/wto/⟩.

Van Der Werf, Martin. 2000. "The Worker Rights Consortium Makes Strides Toward Legitimacy." *Chronicle of Higher Education*. April 21, pp. A41–A42.

Women's Wear Daily. 1996. "Labor Costs: Where and How Much?" December 31. ⟨http://www.nlsearch.com⟩. Accessed 8/12/99.

Worker Rights Consortium. 2000. "WRC Members Schools – 66 Colleges and Universities as of November 20, 2000." ⟨http://www.workersrights.org/members_schools.html⟩.

Worker Rights Consortium. 2000a. "For the Enforcement of University Licensing Codes of Conduct." ⟨http://www.workersrighgts.org/detailed_outline.html⟩.

Worker Rights Consortium. 2000b. "Companion Document." ⟨http://workersrights.org/companion_document.html⟩.

World Bank. 2001. *World Development Indicators 2001*. Washington, DC: World Bank.

World Bank. 1999. *World Development Indicators 1999*. Washington, DC: World Bank.

EIGHT. SAVING GLOBALIZATION

Caribbean Daylight. 2000. "Caribbean Diplomat Speaks Out on Globalization." December 22, p. 24.

Dollar, David, and Aart Kraay. 2000. "Growth *Is* Good for the Poor." World Bank Development Research Group. ⟨www.worldbank.org/research⟩.

Ehrenreich, Barbara. 2000. "Forward." In Sarah Anderson and John Cavanagh, with Thea Lee (eds.), *Field Guide to the Global Economy*. New York: New Press, ix–x.

Faux, Jeff. 1999. "Slouching toward Seattle." *Viewpoints*. ⟨http:www.epinet.org/webfeatures/viewpoints/slouch.html⟩.

Godfrey, Clare. 1998. "A Future for Caribbean Bananas: The Importance of Europe's Banana Market to the Caribbean." ⟨http://www.oxfam.org.uk/policy/papers/bananas.htm⟩.

Greider, William. 2000. "Global Agenda." *Nation*. January 31, pp. 11–16.

Mandle, Jay R. 2001. "Reforming Globalization." *Challenge*. Vol. 44, no. 2 (March–April), 24–38.

Mandle, Jay R. 2000. "The Windward Islands Banana Industry in the Global Economy." *Journal of Eastern Caribbean Affairs*. Vol. 29, no. 4 (December), 1–25.

Nation. 1999. "Free Trade, Fair Trade, Whose Trade? A Forum." December 6, pp. 11–17.

Phillips, Jim 2000. "What Happens after Seattle?" *Dollars and Sense.* No. 227 (January–February), 15–16, 29–32.

Sachs, Jeffrey. 1999. "Helping the World's Poorest." ⟨http://www.cid.harvard.edu/cidsocialpolicy/sf9108.html⟩.

Sanger, David E. 2001. "A Grand Trade Bargain." *Foreign Affairs.* Vol. 80, no. 1 (January–February), 65–75.

Schott, Jeffrey J. 2000. "The WTO after Seattle." In Jeffrey J. Schott (ed.), *The WTO after Seattle.* Washington, DC: Institute for International Economics, 3–40.

United Nations Conference on Trade and Development. 1999. *World Investment Report 1999: Foreign Direct Investment and the Challenge of Development.* New York and Geneva: United Nations.

Williamson, John. 1999. "What Should the Bank Think about the Washington Consensus?" Background paper to the world Bank's *World Development Report 2000.* ⟨http://www.iie.com/testimony/bankwc.htm⟩.

Index

Aaronson, Susan Ariel, 25, 29
Africa, 10, 108
African, Caribbean, and Pacific grouping
    of countries (ACP), 13
African Trade and Development Act of
    2000, 129nl
Agosin, Manuel R., 80
Agreement on Trade-Related Aspects of
    Intellectual Property Rights (TRIPs),
    63
Agreement on Trade-Related Investment
    Measures (TRIMs), 63, 64
agriculture, 49, 113; labor force in,
    109–11, 110t; new technologies in,
    129; protectionism, 14; subsidies, 129
anti-dumping legislation, 35, 128, 131
anti-globalization activists/movement,
    1–3, 37–8, 40–2, 130–1; attitude
    change required in, 131; coalition in,
    29; and FDI mobility, 70; indifference
    to multinational negotiations, 123;
    and Multilateral Agreement on
    Investment, 53–73; viewpoints within,
    3–4, 6, 49–52
anti-modernist attitudes, 130
Antigua, 128
apparel industry: demand for right to
    collective bargaining, 116–17;
    globalization of, 106–14; policing,
    100–6; unions in, 117; working
    conditions in, 100
Apparel Industry Partnership (AIP), 101

Appelbaum, Richard, 103, 104–5
Asia, 10; employment in clothing
    industry, 106; financial crises, 81,
    83–4, 87, 93, 94; labor force in
    agriculture, 109, 111; wages in
    clothing industry, 108, 109, 113
Asian Tigers, 13
Associated Press, 47

Balint, Peter J., 28, 30–1, 34, 37, 53–4,
    68
banana industry, Caribbean, 126–7,
    129–30
Bangladesh, 15, 106, 113
Bank for International Settlements (BIS),
    81, 94
Barbuda, 128
Barlow, Maude, 53, 55–7, 68–9, 70
Bellow, Walden, 50
Bergsten, C. Fred, 36–7
Bhagwati, Jagdish, 14, 46, 86, 93, 98
bilateral investment agreements, 62, 64,
    71
Boeing, 34
Bonacich, Edna, 105
Bordo, Michael D., 11
Borosage, Robert L., 48
bottom-up agreements, 6, 69–73
boycott(s), 68, 114, 116
Brazil, 107; currency devaluation, 81,
    94; poverty level, 23
Bressand, Albert, 58

149